Praise for Open Community

"If you're an association leader, you're already a social media genius. You just need this book to show you how to make it happen."

        Andy Sernovitz, founding CEO, Word of Mouth Marketing Association; author, *Word of Mouth Marketing*

"Community is much more than a buzz word in social media, it is the lifeblood of any organization. Maddie and Lindy offer an incredibly refreshing and approachable book to help you find and connect with the right people to extend your reach today and nurture online communities that work for you."

        Brian Solis, author of *Engage, the complete guide for businesses to build, cultivate, and measure success in the social Web*

"If your association has questions about the best and most effective ways to engage with stakeholders online, Lindy Dreyer and Maddie Grant have provided a clear and helpful guidebook to help you along the way."

        Lisa Junker, CAE, IOM, editor-in-chief, *Associations Now* magazine

"For nonprofits and associations that want to build communities around their work, this book is a must-read for the guiding principles. "

        Beth Kanter, author, *The Networked Nonprofit, using social media to power social networks for change*

"This book provides an invaluable analysis of the strategic, structural, and cultural issues associations using social media face. Leaders can read this book and come out on the other side ready to move, and not because someone ordered them and not because they are desperate to not miss the boat. Awesome."

        Jamie Notter, VP organizational effectiveness, Management Solutions Plus Inc.; author, *We Have Always Done It That Way: 101 Things About Associations We Must Change*

OPEN COMMUNITY

LINDY DREYER & MADDIE GRANT, CAE

A little book of big ideas for associations navigating the social web.

Nobles County Library
407 12th Street
PO Box 1049
Worthington, MN 56187
31315001949952

Copyright © 2010 by Lindy Dreyer and Maddie Grant, CAE

All rights reserved. No part of this book may be reproduced or transmitted in any form or by any means, electronic or mechanical, including photocopying, recording, or by any information storage and retrieval system, without express written permission from the authors.

This book is also available in electronic formats. We tried to convert everything, but some content that appears in print may not be available in electronic books. And it certainly won't be as pretty.

Disclaimer: While the authors have used their best judgement in preparing this book, the ideas being expressed are not guaranteed to work, and may not be suitable for your situation. You should consult with a professional where appropriate. No one involved in writing, editing, cartooning, or publishing this book will be liable for any loss of profit or any other damages of any kind.

Layout by Alison Dixon, founder of ImagePrep Studio. Find her at *http://imageprep.com*

Cartoons by Rob Cottingham, principal at Social Signal and cartoonist extraordinaire behind the Noise to Signal Cartoon. Find him at *http://robcottingham.ca*
All cartoons copyright © 2010 by Rob Cottingham

ISBN: 978-0-9830715-0-1

Printed in the United States of America
Printed by Omnipress in Madison, WI.
http://www.omnipress.com/

Acknowlegements

We have much to be grateful for and many people to thank. First and foremost, to our association community, which has watched us grow from mere geeky babes in the wood into full-fledged digital extroverts. Thank you for letting us test anything and everything through you and for reading, lurking, sharing, responding, tweeting and retweeting, agreeing, pushing back, helping us think harder, providing our sandboxes, being willing to jump in, commiserating, allowing us to rant at times, experimenting with us, asking questions, giving us insanely awesome case studies to write about, and buying us cocktails. And to YAP, our true embodiment of an Open Community, for always dancing.

To Rob Cottingham, who contributed the amazing cartoons in this book, thank you for sharing your talent and your humor with us and our peeps.

To Clay Shirky, Charlene Li, Hugh MacLeod and all of the great authors who have inspired us on a daily basis to continue what you started and delve deep into this conversation.

Speaking of inspiring authors...to Jamie Notter, Beth Kanter, Brian Solis, Lisa Junker, and Andy Sernovitz, thank you for reviewing early versions of this book, giving us your valuable feedback, and letting us know you actually enjoyed reading it. You've given us great hope that others will enjoy reading this, too.

To Dave Sabol, our web guru, and Alison Dixon, our extraordinary graphic designer, thank you for everything you've done behind the scenes to make us who we are.

To Joe Rominiecki, the best editor ever.

To David McKnight and Omnipress for the constant encouragement, and for offering to publish our book right at the time when we were completely stressed with no clue about where to start. You have no idea what a gift that was!

To our families for pushing us to be great, being willing to order pizza when we weren't up for cooking, and doing the dishes during our "computer time."

Introduction
- 10   What this book is.
- 12   What this book isn't.
- 13   Where are the case studies?
- 14   Our truth, so you know where we're coming from.
- 17   Why Open Community?
- 20   Outline of this book.

CHAPTER 1: Open Community Means Collaborating With Purpose.
- 24   Enough with the social media hype already.
- 25   You know your business, but do you know your community?
- 27   Start with people, not tools.
- 28   If you do nothing else, listen and respond.
- 31   Look for strategic thinking from unexpected sources.
- 33   Build your strategy around the sweet spots.
- 34   Work through the secret tug of war.
- 36   Start small and good.
- 37   Simplify complex structures and processes.
- 38   Expect the unexpected, and capitalize on it.
- 39   Fail smart.
- 40   Where's the ROI?
- **42   Get to the point already.**

CHAPTER 2: Open Community Means Developing Into a Social Organization.

46 Don't let old habits get in the way of a strong community.
48 Get used to sharing control.
50 It's about clarity over control.
52 Bust the silos.
53 Ease up on the hierarchies.
57 Establish a good social media policy.
59 Skill sets for a social organization.
62 The role of staff.
63 Who should take part?
64 People interact with people, not organizations.
65 Blurring the line between personal and professional.
67 The new association community manager.
69 Everyone's a publisher.
71 Forget perfect.
73 The time suck.
75 Get to the point already.

CHAPTER 3: Open Community Means Embracing the Ecosystem.

78   There's something to be said for the mess.
80   Understand your role in the ecosystem.
82   Home(base) is where the heart is.
84   Outposts are healthy.
86   Create accidentally-on-purpose spokespersons.
88   All community happens in small groups.
90   Create safe spaces.
92   Public and private spaces can coexist after all.
94   Chapters and components are messy, too.
97   Get to the point already.

CHAPTER 4: Open Community Means Empowering the Periphery.

100   Is there an echo in here?
101   Your community is not your database.
102   Get ready for the Social CRM.
105   Community unlocks more useful data.
106   Behavioral demographics: useful data you already have.
108   From creators to spectators and everything in between.
110   Are they spending time in front of a computer?
111   Generation matters, but not the way you'd think.
113   It's not about age. It's about curiosity.
114   Share the love with your digital extroverts.
115   Find your champions.
117   Who belongs? It's your Open Community's call.
119   Citizens versus members.
120   Get to the point already.

CHAPTER 5: Open Community Means Participant-Defined Engagement.

- 124 Hurdles along the path to engagement.
- 126 Member to member trumps staff to member.
- 128 Schmoozing your champions.
- 130 The role of the champion.
- 131 Getting citizens invested in your organization.
- 133 Adhocracy and Volunteerism 2.0.
- 135 Connect online interactions to face-to-face interactions.
- 137 The simplest thing that could possibly work.
- 139 What's your association's social object?
- 141 Social objects need social actions.
- 143 The "what" trumps the "where."
- 145 Gifts from the community deserve thank-you notes.
- 146 Reputation matters.
- 148 Engagement points and reputation flair.
- **150 Get to the point already.**

Conclusion: Your Community Awaits.

- 154 Your community awaits.
- 156 Appendix
- 159 Endnotes

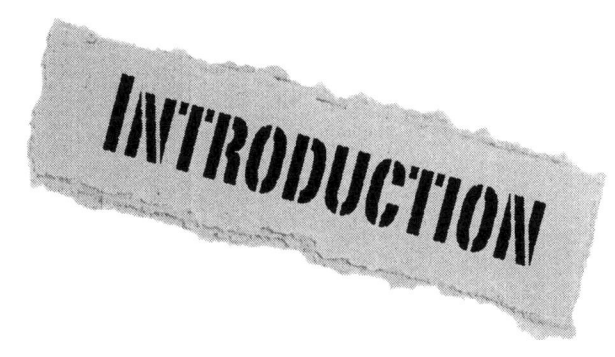

INTRODUCTION

Hey, remind me – what's the keyboard shortcut for creating a vibrant, productive online community?

What this book is.

This book is written for the complicated and quirky world of associations and membership organizations. This book is about how associations can—and why they should—build community online.

Associations all have a mission. They all strive to provide continuing value for the members they represent, whether trade or individual. They all balance the dichotomy between what's good for the order and what's "in it for me as a member." Many associations, being less tied to market forces than for-profit companies, struggle with marrying traditional ways of working with learning to be agile, innovative, and responsive to the changing demographics and technology habits of their members. We come from a marketing (Lindy) and operational (Maddie) background in association management, and we strive in this book to apply our years of experience working in the association industry with our social media experience as industry bloggers, early adopters, and evangelists for all things social. (Or occasionally anti-social, in Lindy's case.)

This little book is a collection of big ideas. These simple yet far-reaching concepts, framed by our own definition of Open Community, describe how to approach the inevitably long and complex process of building community online in such a way as to help your association succeed. We'd love to take credit for all of these ideas, but mostly we just recognize 'em when we see 'em, then adapt the ideas to membership organizations. We don't want you to just take our word for it, which is why we've added a handy reading list in the back of this book in case you're dying to dig in further to any of the concepts we cover.

What this book isn't.

This book is not "Online Community Building for Dummies." And it's not a 101 training manual for social tools. You won't find a list of the best Twitter apps or long discussions about the difference between Facebook groups and pages (if those still exist by the time you read this). If you like that stuff, find us at happy hour—we can talk for hours about it over a cocktail. Instead, we've tried to create a practical, high-level guide for why and how to build community using social media. Most associations are now far enough along in the process of learning about how to use social media from a technical and tactical point of view that there are hundreds of resources available for just that.

This book is also not about building "an online community" or white-label social network. Launching a private social network may be a part of your community special sauce, but when we talk about building your Open Community, we are talking about something much bigger than that. Online community comes in all shapes and sizes and happens in many different places all over the social web. The common denominator is not the tool or site where it's happening but rather the people who are a part of the community.

Where are the case studies?

Everyone loves case studies. You see the problem clearly developed, you see a clear plot that someone followed to confront the problem, and almost always, there's a happy ending. It's Hollywood stuff—*Die Hard with a Briefcase*.

Here's the rub. You cannot achieve Open Community by replicating what someone else is doing. Not to say case studies don't have value. The storytelling is tremendously useful for illustrating tough concepts. For the purposes of this book, we've opted to separate the case studies from the book itself. You can read this book quickly, grab hold of the ideas that resonate most with you, then go to http://opencommunitybook.org where we're busy collecting and blogging about case studies around many of the concepts in this book. And if you have a case study to share with us, we can blog about you, too!

Our truth, so you know where we're coming from.

We accept these six statements as fact. This book is not about proving these points but rather about figuring out how to move forward from here.

1. **It's not about the tools.** Social media tools and public community sites (like Facebook, LinkedIn, Twitter, etc.) continue to change constantly—quite on purpose, as social media by its very nature is responsive and agile and iterative in order to allow consumers to shape the direction and usability of the places where they want to collaborate online. By the time this book is published, some sites we all use today may no longer exist or may look entirely different. An understanding of the key concepts underlying online community should be applicable no matter what specific tools or sites you use to interact with members.

2. **It is about listening and monitoring.** Having a strong and effective internal process for listening and monitoring on the social web is the first step for any organization. This step will tell you how to choose what social sites you need to have a presence in, because those sites are where your community is already convening.

3. **It is about building relationships between people.** Building community online takes time, and it takes personal investment. Yes, personal, not just organizational. An organization cannot build relationships; only the people who work there can. The more you can empower your staff within a safe framework to engage with members and industry stakeholders online, the more your organization can thrive and lead your online community.

4. **It is about understanding the difference between the hub and the spokes.** Building online community today means learning how to navigate between outpost activity (on public sites like Facebook) and homebase activity (on your own website, white-label community space, or blog). We'll dig into how different social spaces relate to each other and how your organizational presence might change accordingly.

5. **It is about tending the garden.** Open Communities need to be nurtured. Members need to be clear on what the community is for and what they can do inside it. The needs of a member as she moves from newbie (new to the online community) to champion (experienced user willing to welcome the next wave of newbies) changes over time. An organization has a very important community-management role to play to help its online community grow, help it become self-sustaining, help it adjust as its members' needs change, and of course, help it stay aligned with the overall mission of the association.

6. **It is about clarity over control.** This is a big one—an overarching theme that extends into everything we've written and everything we've learned about building community on the social web. Organizations are moving away from a mechanistic, top-down "system" into an organic, messy, evolving "ecosystem" because of social media. The way that organizations can continue to be mission-driven within this context is by being very clear about why they exist and how social media can help—by being very clear about the goals of social activity and how each person (staff or member) has a role to play in that. This theme will come up again and again throughout this book.

Why Open Community?

To understand why Open Community is important, we need to define what we're talking about here. After all, there are as many definitions of community as there are communities defining community. (Phew!) Sociologists say one thing. Ethnographers say something else. Biologists have another definition. The concept of Open Community encompasses the myriad ways that community manifests online. Here is how we define Open Community for the purposes of this book:

> **Open Community** *(noun)*
> A diverse group of people, bonded by a common interest in an industry and an organization, who care enough to contribute and cooperate online for the good of the group.[1]

Notice there is nothing in there about geography? That's because Open Community can be completely separate from traditional ideas of communities bound by location. Where once communities needed only be broad enough to include people who could be geographically present, niche online communities can now bond people from all over the world.

Notice there is nothing in there about membership? That's because the word membership has a lot of business-model connotations for association executives. Open Community extends beyond the member database to potential members, nonmembers, and others in a diverse community ecosystem. You might also notice some touchy-feely words in there. For example, we use the word *bonded*. Communities have a special kind of connectedness that goes beyond simply joining a group. We also use the words *care*, *contribute*, and *cooperate*. Being a part of the community really means something to these folks, so much so that they are willing to give of themselves and their time to shape the community for the better.

So back to the question at hand: why build Open Community? Because the Internet makes community scalable, visible, and measurable. Because if you don't, someone else will. Because associations are community experts and uniquely positioned to contribute meaningfully. Associations can now:

- Remove obstacles (like geography) that used to keep people from contributing.

- Enable more types of contributions.

- Help people cooperate with one another both synchronously and asynchronously.

- Find and invite thought leaders from the periphery of their memberships and their industries or from other industries altogether.

- Reflect the richness of their offline, face-to-face member communities in the online environment (and make a good impression on prospective members).

Ultimately, you'll need to answer the *why* for your own organization, if you haven't already. **The big ideas in this little book will help you refine your *why* and add a little *how*.**

Outline of this book.

We called this book a "little book of big ideas" because it's meant to introduce some simple yet essential concepts for building Open Community that are actionable and applicable to any association, large or small. The beauty of the association industry is that we all have certain management issues in common, yet each association has its own quirkiness, its own personality, its own way of doing things. We believe in the mantra "start with the simplest thing that could possibly work," and we've applied it to this book as well. We hope that the concepts here will be easy enough to modify and replicate at any association.

The book itself is organized around five overarching ideas, one per chapter.

1. Open Community means collaborating with purpose.
2. Open Community means developing into a social organization.
3. Open Community means embracing the ecosystem.
4. Open Community means empowering the periphery.
5. Open Community means participant-defined engagement.

Chapter 1: Open Community means collaborating with purpose.
The first chapter gives you a simple framework for figuring out how to define your Open Community strategy by starting with listening on the social web, identifying your stakeholders' online behaviors and where they hang out, aligning individual business goals with organizational strategy, and measuring what matters to achieve success.

Chapter 2: Open Community means developing into a social organization.
The next chapter covers specific ideas for building internal organizational capacity to build and nurture Open Community, including how to prepare for the impact of social media on your internal processes, individual behaviors, and organizational culture.

Chapter 3: Open Community means embracing the ecosystem.
The third chapter describes the messy ecosystem of your open community: the relationship between the public social sites where your stakeholders are already hanging out and the homebase you want to attract them into, what to do about accidental spokespersons, and the importance of small groups.

Chapter 4: Open Community means empowering the periphery.
The fourth chapter discusses how to think about your people differently, in terms of the engagement lifecycle from newbie to champion, the rise of digital extroverts, the member as citizen, and how to find your champions.

Chapter 5: Open Community means participant-defined engagement.
You've built your online villages, you've opened the doors, now what? What are your members actually going to *do* once they

get there? In the final chapter, we explain the concept of the social object and why that is crucial to the success of your Open Community. We'll give you some simple tips for seeding and nurturing your community, too.

You can skip around all you like, but really, we hope we've created an airplane book—easily digestible in one sitting and interesting enough to keep reading through the Dramamine-induced drowsiness. Hey—we fly into DCA all the time ... a girl's gotta do what a girl's gotta do.

Open Community Means Collaborating With Purpose

As a matter of fact, the Delicious feed I set up is updating our Posterous site, which populates our association's WordPress blog. So I'm actually really very busy.

Enough with the social media hype already.

What's all this social media stuff really worth for your organization? "Being Social," "crowdsourcing," "socialnomics," "the attention economy," "the relationship economy"—the buzz words are everywhere. Everyone's talking about this social media stuff—it might even be getting irritating to you. (It is to us, and we live and breathe it!) You may wish you could just ignore it, but you're smart and you know that's not an option. You also know that just using social media for the sake of having a Facebook Page or a Twitter account just doesn't make sense. There has to be a real, "show me the ROI" reason to start and some business intelligence backing that up.

So forget the hype. Social media is useless unless your association can use it efficiently and deliberately to get where you need to go. Think of it like this: your objective is the destination, your strategy is the map to get to that destination, social media tools are a vehicle, and your community is what powers the whole system. And let's face it, without a vibrant community backing you up, you're never going to get very far.

You know your business, but do you know your community?

Building community online doesn't have to be complicated, but it does take work. It also takes courage, knowing that you're going to put your organization out there without knowing exactly how everything will unfold. You're used to being able to predict the results of the work you do. You know your business—maybe too well. You may have a hard time seeing the possibilities created by online community. Or, you may see so many possibilities that you can't clearly see the easy wins and first steps.

It's hard to step back, to see the big picture, when all you're thinking is, how do we start harnessing all this conversation? How do we embrace the messiness of community in a way that makes strategic sense for the organization, in a way that is mission driven? We have unofficial Facebook groups, we're on LinkedIn, some of our staff are active on Twitter, maybe we should build our own homebase now. How do we make sense of it all? How do we give it direction?

" *It's easy to get caught up in the way you've always done business, closing yourself off from possibilities that may very well supplant those business processes.* "

And it's easy to get caught up in the way you've always done business, closing yourself off from possibilities that may very well supplant those business processes. Moving toward a more social model of running an association stretches us. It tests our patience, and it's crazy scary. But when you really get a handle on your community–when you really know who they are, what they need, where to find them, how to get them talking, how to get them acting collectively–you learn what you're doing right and what you need to change, and you make more intelligent business decisions.

Start with people, not tools.

Know your members, know your members, know your members. Do not assume you know what "tools" you need or what social spaces your stakeholders are hanging out in based on demographics alone. In fact, never start by choosing the tools first ("we need a blog," "we should be on Facebook," "we should build our own community platform," etc.). Figure out where people are talking about you in social spaces. Figure out where your members already are, where your competitors' members are, where your potential members are. You need to continually learn about your members and stakeholders and the kinds of social media activities they prefer. Getting to know your members and stakeholders online is covered much more in Chapter 4.

Having a good understanding of the people who are (or will be) a part of your online community will help you set realistic expectations for what you can accomplish in terms of bringing your community together, choosing the right tools, and achieving your business objectives.

If you do nothing else, listen and respond.

If you need a starting place, here it is. Build the capacity to listen and respond to your community as an organization. No matter what, *do not skip this step.*

"Listening" on the social web can start simply—at its most basic, it just means searching the web for relevant keywords like your association's name, industry keywords, key people, and your sister (or competitor) organizations. Make sure you test keywords in good ol' Google first, and pay attention to the "advanced search" operators. Once you are comfortable that your search results are bringing up relevant stuff for you, you can set up Google Alerts which can come in to your email or RSS reader automatically every time someone mentions one of your keywords online. Search public sites like Facebook, LinkedIn, and Twitter, too. In the beginning, you don't actually need to have a profile in most of these spaces to search for industry terms and to see if anyone out there is already talking.

Ideally, the work of listening on the social web should be done by several people. In the same way that eight people at a dinner party will hear different conversations swirling around the table, eight people setting up Google alerts will get different results based on the keywords they choose—and that's a good thing. Getting those folks together to compare notes on a regular basis will give you a good grasp on the big picture. As for who that listening team should be? A member of your communications and PR department may already be monitoring your brand in social media spaces. (If not, they should be!) Along with your PR expert, try to find someone willing to help from each of several different departments. Eventually, listening on the social web is something that almost everyone in an organization should be comfortable doing.

Through your listening efforts, you'll start to see where people are talking about you or your industry. Assess the situation. Are your members getting started without you? (This is likely.) Are they forming their own groups around your organization, brand, or industry? Are they asking for more? Is there a fair amount of activity in several places already, but no coherent strategy? Do you just know you need to do something, but you're not sure what? Create an inventory of both official and unofficial social spaces that host your community members. Find out if any of your staff are actively monitoring or participating in those spaces. If they are, great. If not, find someone willing to put in the effort.

" *Eight people at a dinner party will hear different conversations swirling around the table, just like eight people setting up Google alerts will get different results based on the keywords they choose—* " *and that's a good thing.*

And most importantly, figure out how to respond to people who are talking about you. Discuss how your staff and key volunteers can safely interact in those communities. Responding can be as simple as correcting the date of an event or thanking someone for their support—or, in very rare cases, it can be as nuanced and politically charged as a crisis communications effort. Build social media into your PR crisis communications plan and know who the most appropriate employees and volunteers are in each social site who could respond to an escalated conversation.

The inventory we mentioned above? That should list the names of the admin person, active staff people, and most influential members in any social network you've identified. Associations that actively build community in online spaces place a huge amount of trust in their staff and members, and they work every day to continue to build and nurture that trust, even through setbacks.

Look for strategic thinking from unexpected sources.

Set up a brainstorming session and lay everything out on the table. Get everyone in the room who has thoughts or ideas on what they want to do related to online community and social media. Make sure different departments are represented, as well as different levels of seniority and experience. Invite the naysayers alongside the devoted social media practitioners. Devote several hours to talking about every aspect you can think of. What would be nice to have, what would be necessary? What are the fears? Should your communities have more public (open) spaces or more private (closed) spaces? What is your comfort level for conversation with your stakeholders, as opposed to just marketing to them? Talk about goals for building community online from each department's point of view. Write down everyone's ideas. You might end up with something like this:

- Publications wants to get better feedback on topics of interest to members and be able to crowdsource expertise from a larger percentage of the membership.

- Meetings wants to build buzz for the annual conference.

- Legal wants to be able to watch for possible anti-trust situations and stem that risk before it happens.

- Marketing wants to promote new programs better and in a more targeted way.
- Public Relations wants to position the association as a source of the most up-to-date information on hot issues.
- Government Relations wants to encourage grassroots advocacy in new ways to support the association's members.
- Membership wants to attract younger members, for example people in their final years of study in the association's field.
- Communications wants to find ways to collaborate better internally and with volunteers.
- Development wants to find ways to raise money creatively and using methods that leverage the viral nature of social media.

Build your strategy around the sweet spots.

Once you've done this brainstorming, it should be possible to group departmental objectives so that perhaps a few overall organizational objectives emerge. Prioritize and synthesize. We like to stick with three achievable goals. Based on a myriad of individual departmental objectives like those we illustrated above, perhaps they could be grouped liked this:

- To establish the organization as a thought leader in the industry.

- To attract younger members in a variety of ways.

- To enable "drop in" volunteerism so members can participate in the activities of the organization in they way that THEY want to.

Then find the sweet spots. You might have a hot topic that touches many different departments and many facets of your member community. You might have shared goals that cross departments. You might have multiple sources of content that could flow together to help you reach one of your goals. Play on the strengths you already have, even as you look for new competencies you need to build.

Work through the secret tug of war.

Even if your strategy process goes great—you get tons of great ideas and energy from everyone involved—beware of the secret tug of war going on behind the scenes.

> **On the one side, you have the skeptics who simply can't see how any of this will ever actually work. On the other side, you have the enthusiasts who are chomping at the bit to get going.**

On the one side, you have the skeptics who simply can't see how any of this will ever actually work. They're convinced that you are sinking too much time and too much energy into something only a small group of people will ever use. They are focused on the risks and the disruption of all of the carefully constructed processes your association has always relied upon.

On the other side, you have the enthusiasts who are chomping at the bit to get going and don't understand what's taking so long. They're convinced that social media tools are the future and they can't be bothered to think about the risks or the bigger picture implications for the association. They're likely already experimenting with some social media projects, and everything is going just fine, thank you very much.

You will get nowhere fast without being aware of these two personalities and finding a way to bring them along for the ride. With patience, small wins, and good story gathering, skeptics can be convinced over time. Hard core enthusiasts are tougher, believe it or not, because they can't spare the time. They may feel like you're holding them back and leave. But hopefully, you can mentor them along by helping them understand how the business objectives of the organization need to guide everything they do.

Start small and good.

Now you can choose your toolset. Once you've done your listening and figured out your most important objectives, you will be able to determine what tools (and there often will be more than one) will help you achieve them.

Then it's time to experiment. Start small. We always say that small and good can lead to large and good, but large and bad is a lost cause. (A reckless rewording of Gall's Law[2], possibly inspired by Clay Shirky.) Learn from what you are doing, readjust all the time, benchmark and measure your progress. You can learn a lot by experimenting in different ways, seeing what works and what doesn't, what engages members and builds community and what falls flat.

Associations that are really good at experimenting have a framework in place for embracing and implementing new ideas from staff and volunteers at all levels. They ask the right questions at the right times. Questions like:

- What are you trying to accomplish?
- Why this tool?
- Who is it for and how will you get them to use it?
- Who will moderate and track the progress?
- What does success look like?

Simplify complex structures and processes.

Resist the urge to use social tools to recreate the business processes and organizational structures you created back when group forming and communication was hard—it's not hard anymore. In fact, spend some time daydreaming what your association might look like if you started it today using only social tools. Would you still have incorporated chapters? What would your governance structure look like? How would you publish your magazine, newsletters, and journals? What might peer review look like? What special interest groups would spring up? Are they the same as the ones you have now? How would your local and national events be different?

Before social tools, we needed complex structures and processes to make the work discrete and manageable for administrators. But in online social spaces, complexity means confusion—about what to join, where to click, how to post, how to follow along. And the more steps or features you add (even when the steps used to make sense), the more likely you will dissuade someone from participating.

Expect the unexpected, and capitalize on it.

As you build community online, you may begin to notice unexpected opportunities, things you didn't plan for but that you know you can capitalize on. Is a part of your community discussing a new trend that they need to learn more about, but no one is providing that training? Provide it. Is there are group of members creating great, substantive content that members need? Publish it. Are market changes causing your community to intersect with a different community you've never served before? Serve it.

> *Before calling an effort a failure, look for the unexpected gains and achievements and see if they make it all worthwhile.*

Part of the beauty (and the frustration) of online community is the organic (chaotic) ebb and flow of people and conversations that you can only influence so much. The business objectives you thought you could achieve might not be the business objectives that you are achieving. Before calling an effort a failure, look for the unexpected gains and achievements and see if they make it all worthwhile.

Fail smart.

The cost of failure is very low (at least when you're talking about public social spaces), and it's perfectly OK to try things and abandon those that require too much effort or those that are just not working well. With the tools and possibilities evolving as fast as they are, trial and error is a legitimate research tool as you work to match your community's needs. The keys are that you truly know your members and stakeholders and that you have determined your organizational, strategic objectives. Then you can judge whether things are working (or failing) by measuring and benchmarking against your objectives.

And the faster you fail, the faster you can move on to the next experiment. Of course, if you hope to be able to continue experimenting, you need to be sure you are setting realistic expectations with your board and your leadership. Explain that failure is actually built into your process, and set the bar low with each small effort. That way, when you succeed, your accomplishments will be all the more appreciated.

Also, find a way to prepare your staff and volunteers for the possibility of failure. And when a project doesn't work out, separate the failure from the staff and volunteers who poured their heart and soul into the effort. Be prepared to harness their energy into a project that is succeeding so they can renew their optimism.

Where's the ROI?

The ROI question is always looming, right? Return on investment is an important business measurement, and while there are a million ways to measure social media, there is no easy way to measure the ROI of your online community. We see two ways to approach ROI when discussing social media with your board and leadership.

The first approach (and admittedly a cop-out) is that online community is not so much a tactic to measure as it is a new way of working with our members and stakeholders. As associations, a big part of our job is to provide leadership and solid relationships with influential industry leaders; when social media becomes a communications hub for those leaders, the association has no choice but to use it. What's the ROI of good phone skills? Or email etiquette? For this argument to be effective, you need to be able to show broad adoption of social media communication by influential members. Your listening efforts should make that simple enough.

> *Find the most analytical person you have and ask him or her to design a method for benchmarking and tracking your online community. Start with your objectives.*

The second approach is measuring what matters. Find the most analytical person you have—perhaps someone with a strong marketing or research background—and ask him or her to design a method for benchmarking and tracking your online community. Start with your objectives. How would you know if you're meeting those objectives? What can you easily measure to prove it? What's harder to measure and might require some qualitative research? Your board and leadership will appreciate success stories and testimonials more than they will appreciate a "25 percent increase in retweets from the second quarter."

GET TO THE POINT ALREADY.

- Why would you use social media? To meet your business objectives, of course. Only, you can't reasonably do that without some kind of strategy to guide you and help you match the right tools to achievable objectives. And it's all useless without a vibrant online community fueling your efforts.

- So forget the hype and the buzzwords and focus on the people. Get to know your community where they are already interacting online. Learn the tools they use, their online behaviors, and how you as an organization can listen and respond in a way that will continually build trust between you and your community.

- Work collaboratively across silos and hierarchies to identify the possibilities social media holds for your association. Identify shared business objectives and sweet spots where your staff and volunteers can make the best use of existing resources, even as you identify emerging needs. Work patiently and tirelessly to bring along the skeptics and guide the enthusiasts.

- Welcome new social media ideas, even as you filter them through a strategic lens. Start small and good and experiment regularly. Plan for failure and learn from it. Set reasonable expectations with your board and leadership (not to mention your staff and volunteers). And be ready to respond to the ROI question, either by proving broad adoption by key influencers or by measuring what matters to prove you are reaching your objectives.

CHAPTER 2

Open Community Means Developing Into a Social Organization

After being exposed to those mutating cosmic rays, my career options were super-villain or social media manager.

Don't let old habits get in the way of a strong community.

Now, so we know what we're trying to do with our social media efforts, and we've chosen the places we'd like to start experimenting. But how do we actually start doing this work? How do we start to integrate it into our normal workflow?

A strong Open Community will demand a more social organization. A social organization is more transparent with its community, sharing information as freely as is strategically viable. A social organization is more decentralized, empowering staff on all levels to do what is necessary to best serve the community. A social organization is more fearless, trusting the inherent goodwill of the community, even in the face of criticism or a bad experience. A social organization is also more collaborative—this is critical. The social organization works collaboratively both internally and externally to get work done. It naturally seeks the guidance of the community when a problem arises that can not be easily solved. It constantly interfaces with community members along the way.

> **social organization** *(noun)*
> An organization with a structure, processes, and culture that embrace the social media principles of openness and decentralization as a means to achieve strategic business goals.

This is not an all-or-nothing scenario. You can have a very powerful community without embracing all of the traits of a social organization. But most associations that seek to build community online will need to do some soul searching and evolve in three important ways:

1. Build awareness of individual behaviors, because everyone must take personal responsibility for their ability to collaborate with each other, interact with the community, and become more comfortable with social tools.
2. Change internal processes, because building (and managing) Open Community demands collaboration across departments and hierarchies.
3. Shift the organizational culture, because a strong Open Community will interact with nearly everyone in your organization, not just your top leadership, and your culture will have a huge impact on the quality of those interactions.

Get used to sharing control.

There are two myths of control out there that we need to debunk. The first myth is that by not engaging in social media, you can maintain much more control over your brand, your message, your member database, or your employee's behavior and interactions. Not true. Never was true, but since communication used to be slower and one way, we had the illusion of control, even as our fans and critics formed their own opinions behind our backs. Now the pace of communication is faster (and accelerating all the time), and our fans and critics have a platform where they can spread their opinions far and wide to your community, with or without you.

" *A second myth is that you now have no control. Not true. You are, in essence, sharing control with the people who talk about you.* "

Which brings us to the second myth: that you now have no control. Not true. Along the "best defense is a good offense" train of thought, you can do remarkable things that make your association stand out—stuff that people want to talk about. You can lead the way and share the spotlight with your fans (and sometimes your critics) so that the entire community benefits. You are, in essence, sharing control with the people who talk about you, which is better than ceding control all together.

Building community online may feel like being out of control at first. But the more vibrant your community, the more people you know who will come to your defense in the face of criticism. The more people you know who will spread the content and essence of your organization. The more people you know who believe in your association and your leadership. That's a whole new kind of control, and your community is the safety net.

It's about clarity over control.

"Clarity over control" is the key to leading the way and sharing the spotlight. When we talk about clarity, we're really just asking that you define in simple terms how building community will advance your mission, just like you would define how any other kind of work advances your mission.

> **clarity over control** *(noun)*
> A leadership concept in which the clear articulation of an organization's most important priorities, universally understood by all stakeholders at all levels of the organization, de-emphasizes the need for centralized control over every detail of the organization's activities.

Internally, clarity means that everyone knows:

- The business objectives for building community online.
- Who will be doing what, based on an inventory of activities, sites, and responsibilities.
- How staff will communicate what they hear on the social web.

- How and when responses are handled or escalated when necessary.
- How to propose new projects.
- How online activity relates to offline activity and what particular business timelines are relevant.

Clarity for managing new individual behaviors and skill sets means each employee will be able to answer:

- What is my role in online social spaces and in the community?
- How can I build online relationships personally and professionally, and how do I draw the line between the two?
- How much of my time should I be spending online, and how will I know if I'm making progress?
- Who is in charge of the social media and community efforts, and how do I fit in?

Clarity from an organizational standpoint means everyone will understand:

- What are the benefits for the association and the industry?
- What are the risks to always bear in mind (HIPPA, antitrust, etc.)?
- Who are your members, and how does that affect your interactions online?

- What information can you share freely with members?

Now, we know that achieving clarity may not be as simple as all that. But we also know you already have a mission or vision statement of some kind, even if it's badly written. Start with that. Distill that down to why your association exists and how building community online can help you achieve those reasons for existing.

Bust the silos.

People often talk about the "myth of control" in terms of messaging and marketing. But control runs far deeper than that in most associations. Control goes hand in hand with department silos. Control goes hand in hand with turf wars. The only way to start breaking down walls between departments is to create a process and internal framework where departments have to talk to each other (and work together) on a regular basis. Building community online is great for this, since every department can identify objectives that could be achieved with the community. Just by identifying those individual objectives and figuring out the crossover and collaborative sweet spots that will move you toward your broader, organizational objectives, you are already beginning to bust those silos.

> *Control goes hand in hand with department silos. Control goes hand in hand with turf wars.*

Whether you start by hiring a full-time community manager or setting up an internal, interdepartmental social media team, you will find that the person or people responsible for managing your organization's social media activities will inevitably be talking to many others within the organization.

The team is likely to have several "task forces" which bring in relevant people for particular focus areas.

- The listening and monitoring task force might bring in your PR team.

- The social media policy task force might (make that *should*) bring in your legal team.

- The task force planning social media activities around your annual conference might bring in your event planning and marketing teams.

- The task force overseeing a particularly vibrant LinkedIn group (or Facebook page, or Twitter account) might bring in people from your job board or young-professional teams.

Giving all of these people a central place to talk to each other, work out thorny issues, upload documents, and revisit the main objectives or policies at any time is a good idea and will go a long way towards breaking down internal divisions. When everyone can align their activities with overall organizational goals, they can see that no matter what the specifics are that they are working on, everything relates to the mission.

Ease up on the hierarchies.

Open Community breaks down vertical hierarchies in two ways. First, a strong community will likely interact with staff they know professionally without necessarily being sensitive to their level within the organization. And second, it makes sense to use the talents of staff members who are comfortable in social spaces as part of the social media task forces and in the day-to-day work of listening and responding to the community. These may be younger staff members or people who happen to be great with providing shareable content—taking photos at your conference and uploading them to Flickr, for example.

More often than not, the people who are best positioned to do the day-to-day work of listening, posting, and interacting with the community are lower in the organizational hierarchies we've created. That's because many of the daily tasks are tactical by nature and fit very will within the skill sets of lower-level staff who are already involved with publishing content, member services, or PR monitoring, for example. And yet, the people who are best positioned to provide the strategic guidance to make the work matter are higher in the organizational hierarchies. That doesn't sound so different from any other type of work—except for one thing. Your online community expects two-way communication and a level of responsiveness that can not be achieved with hierarchical approval processes and rules.

Which means that the social media team needs to include people from all levels of the hierarchy, and the people in leadership positions need to find ways to welcome perspectives from the middle and the lower levels of the hierarchy. Clarity over control is the key to changing the process and building the capacity to respond quickly to your community's needs, and it all starts with open, consistent dialogue.

Establish a good social media policy.

A social media policy is key to providing staff with clarity about how they can interact with your community online. We've worked with staff who were very reluctant to do any work online without a policy to answer their key questions:

- How am I supposed to represent myself?
- What are the risks I need to avoid?
- What kind of information am I allowed to put out there?
- What happens if I make a mistake?
- Who do I go to if I have a question or problem?

The policy becomes more than just a set of rules. It's a living document that can be used as a training tool to help staff who are using social tools understand the organization's expectations of them. It's also a tool to help you bring along the skeptics in your organization. If they feel comfortable with the policy, they may take another step along the path with you.

Finally, the policy is a strategic tool that can start the evolution toward a more social organization. When the leaders of the organization adopt good policies, they are creating a safe environment for their staff to experiment with being more open, more collaborative, more fearless. And as your strategy for building community online evolves, your social media policies may need to evolve as well to enable staff to do what needs to be done.

Skill sets for a social organization.

New skill sets are needed for your association to become a social organization—but luckily these are easy to learn and there are lots of resources out there. You'll go far just by doing and experimenting, too.

- **Listening.** Everyone in a social organization should be comfortable with listening, both with online search tools and through their community relationships. You'll need some search-engine ninjas, RSS-reader Jedi masters, and Twitter superheros. And you'll need people flexible and skilled enough to learn the next great listening tool when it arrives.

- **Content curation.** You'll learn through experimentation what kinds of content work best for your community, but no matter what, we're all figuring out how to create bite-sized pieces of content that can be posted on Facebook and shared on Twitter. Blogs are a great way to play with multimedia by mixing up different kinds of posts with photos, videos, audio clips. You can do this internally with a private blog if you're not comfortable (yet) with setting up an association blog.

- **Conversation.** This may seem odd to include as a skill set, but many people have an innate fear of taking part in conversations online for the first time, especially staff responding on behalf of the organization. Your policies will help set up the framework for people to understand the purpose of engaging in conversations, but it may also be helpful to look at examples of online conversations and discuss how one might take part.

- **Social etiquette.** Who do you friend? How do you fit in with the community zeitgeist? How frequently should you update? How nuanced should your security and privacy settings be? All of these questions are part of the skill set that will separate the staff that thrive and make solid connections with your community's social spaces from the staff that come across as awkward, spammy, or even rude.

- **Facilitating and mediating.** Being able to facilitate connections between people in the community is an important skill. Along similar lines, being able to effectively mediate disagreements between people in your community is important to creating the safe space your community needs. The trick is learning to facilitate and mediate in the open, where it can be observed publicly.

- **Collaboration.** Having strong collaboration skills is essential, not only in collaborating with the community but also in collaborating with fellow staff. Open Community is a moving target. The only constant is change. Collaboration skills are the key to facing and managing change, to working through it without sacrificing the strength and security of the organization.

The role of staff.

An important part of building your Open Community is taking part as members of the community. Even if members prefer to interact with each other, staff can play a key role in facilitating those interactions. You'll want to think about the many ways your staff can engage, at different levels and from different departments. Staff can and should:

- Welcome new members into the community spaces.
- Thank members for their contributions.
- Listen and discuss the community's latest trending topics with other staff.
- Promote especially good content and discussions from the community in other association communications.
- Make content on your website more easily shareable within the online community.
- Do cool stuff that gets the community talking.
- Use events to connect your face-to-face community with your online community.
- Go wherever the community takes you—from Facebook to Twitter to Foursquare to the next big thing, whatever that may be.

Who should take part?

In the early stages of building community online, anyone who feels comfortable engaging members online should be empowered to do so. It doesn't matter what department they are from. It doesn't matter how junior or senior they are. All the work you do to provide clarity—clear objectives and strategy, your policies, staff training, collaboration across the organization—should enable anyone with the desire to take part.

Ideally your association will progress to the point where, if a staff member interacts with members face to face, he or she also interacts with members online. The social web is just an additional way to talk to members. Having said that, interacting online requires some newer skills that take time to build. You'll need to provide some training.

You may well have staff who have zero offline interaction with members but are very comfortable online and have an interest in interacting with your community. You'll need to provide some training for them as well. You might try the buddy system—pairing a digital newbie who has member communications skills with a member-facing newbie who has digital social skills.

People interact with people, not organizations.

Your staff represent the organization, but they are also real people. And as real people, they have the ability to build relationships within the community based on authentic, personal interactions. It's a whole lot more difficult to blindly criticize an organization when you personally know the people who work there. Equally, it's easier to compliment someone you see as a real person. Ideally, staff should be considered individuals with personalities of their own who are just as much a part of the community as the rest of the people in it.

So what happens when someone from your staff becomes a superstar in your community? It's bound to happen. There will be certain people who know everyone or become well known because of their responsiveness or their great content curation. And there's a good chance that person won't be the executive director or the head of marketing, though they will be working closely and collaboratively across the organization. Want to really freak yourself out? What if your superstar leaves!?

A social organization is always cultivating the next superstar to take over. It's a good idea to have your superstar think about his or her own succession—in case he or she gets sick or goes on maternity leave or gets called into service by POTUS. (You really can't say no to the President.)

Blurring the lines between personal and professional.

Even as individuals get more savvy about online privacy, a cultural shift is blurring the boundaries between personal and professional interactions in online communities. Take Twitter, for example. Here is a space where individuals are expected to show some personality and have authentic interactions with their peers. For some people, that means sharing a photograph of every gourmet meal they eat with their foodie friends, alongside links about their industry for their professional friends, alongside calls to donate to their favorite charity, alongside updates when they arrive at their favorite Irish pub. People are complicated. Their online identity reflects that.

> " *Social organizations have an astounding ability to trust in their staff, probably because they work so hard to be clear about expectations.* "

Ultimately, your staff has the right to decide how much of their personal lives is exposed to the public, to Google, and thus to your members. It will be up to each individual to take responsibility for the intersection of his or her work life and personal life online.

Equally, your organization has the right to draw the line somewhere. Most of us have employee conduct policies; these same principles can and should extend to online spaces. And it's the job of the organization to communicate what's expected of employees who are interacting in our professional community. It's also our job to make good hiring choices, selecting people who show good judgment online without discriminating based on their personal affiliations.

At the end of the day, it all comes down to trust. Social organizations have an astounding ability to trust in their staff, probably because they work so hard to be clear about expectations.

The new association community manager.

Trust is especially paramount when hiring a community manager who will be responsible for daily interactions in online environments. Community Manager is not a new title within associations. What's changed, then, is the nature of the community and the skill set needed to manage it. While we believe that community management should be part of every member-facing staffer's role, we see a huge benefit for associations that can hire a community manager to lead the charge and coordinate efforts—someone who is especially comfortable online, both personally and professionally, and can be a model for other staff to emulate. This is a full-time gig. On a day-to-day basis, the community manager would:

- Provide strategic direction, tactical expertise, and cross-department coordination for new social media initiatives.

- Listen on behalf of the organization to online conversations and trends, triage, and report what they hear back to the leadership.

- Advocate for members of the online community and make sure their individual voices and feedback are heard.

- Evangelize (and train staff) within the organization on using social tools and concepts to continue building and nurturing the online community.
- Keep track of official outposts and homebase activity.
- Identify unofficial outposts the organization can partner with.
- Measure success, both quantitative and qualitative, so that the association's leadership and board of directors can understand the value of the community.

A lot of associations will begin building their community online before hiring a community manager, instead relying on a team of individuals who are already doing some of the real-life community management to begin to do their work online. This is a legitimate tactic, but at some point—especially in organizations with a lot of members online and organizations with large staffs—a full-time community manager can be an invaluable resource servicing the entire organization. A good community manager enables staff and volunteers alike to interact more effectively with your Open Community.

Everyone's a publisher.

Along the lines of enabling staff and volunteers to do what needs to be done, one of those jobs is publishing. Not only the traditional kinds of publishing we're used to but also new-media publishing, which emphasizes speed, conversational context, and micro-formats like Twitter and Facebook updates. This new kind of publishing will likely involve staff who have never been part of the publishing or communications department but who might be willing to help spread the organization's content and messages in large and small ways. Which is great, because to keep up, organizations need all hands on deck.

Before the Internet, publishing was really hard. Now it's easy. Crazy easy. Many associations are built around the ability to find and publish content from experts, from members, from proprietary research, and so on. When you're building your community online, keep in mind that every person in your community can be their own publisher and can build a significant following. You have two options to maintain your knowledge leadership. One, publish better, faster, more. Two, curate what your community members are publishing. Most associations will find a balance between these two options.

You might ask, "What about all of our private, peer-reviewed, or premium content that's behind the member login on our website?" That's the million-dollar question. There can still be value in knowledge and information but only if that information cannot be found faster and and cheaper (or for free) through a simple Google search.

Do the Google test. When Google is your competition, how do you redefine the value of your information? What do you have hidden behind your login that could help you compete with free resources and improve your ranking in search results? What can you give away to your community, in the spirit of openness and collaboration, that will energize them around your organization? What can you give away that will make the more unique, exclusive, paid content that much more appealing?

The second part of the Google test is this: What do you have that is truly unique and thus well worth the price? Are you charging enough? It's a great idea to always consider how you can cut up your deeper content into bite-sized pieces (blog posts, summaries, videos, charts and graphs) that your community can share and discuss far and wide and then come back to you for the meat.

Forget perfect.

"The perfect is the enemy of the good." —Voltaire[3]

In this digital age where everyone is a publisher, it's more important to be fast than to be letter-perfect. Focus on speed and value—the most sharable content, the nuggets of information that will get people talking—rather than making sure every sentence is exactly right. The editors out there are cringing. (So is Lindy!) But in this social world, overthinking every detail can bring your content stream to a screeching halt. You may actually be stripping all personality out of the content you are providing, which means it runs the risk of being boring and therefore unshareable. That's the last thing you want.

To be clear, we're not advocating that you accept factually or technically incorrect information as a necessary evil. The nature of your organization will dictate the extent to which you can accept errors. Some scientific, technical, or research-oriented associations may choose to sacrifice speed for the sake of accuracy. So long as you're intentional about your publishing strategy and clear about what kinds of errors you must avoid, you're moving in a good direction.

Leaving behind perfect in favor of speed means you might make more mistakes, both as individuals and as the organization. This is where the fearlessness comes back into play. You have to be willing to accept some setbacks to thrive, especially in the beginning as people are working to get used to operating in this new way.

Leaving behind perfect can also create collaboration. Maybe you don't have all of the details, but you have enough that you need to get the information out there. Your community can help you fill in where you leave off.

And when your community values open dialogue, leaving behind perfect is essential. Instead, focus on getting the right people into the conversations as quickly as possible.

The time suck.

Every organization just starting out worries about the "time suck," and there is no doubt that building community online takes time and effort. They also worry about who is going to do this work. In a social organization, building community online is everyone's job, with certain people (like your community manager) spending more time because it impacts their work to a greater degree. This is another area where providing clarity is crucial. Your staff needs to get their jobs done, whatever they are. In one scenario, the community might help them be more efficient or effective. In another scenario, they could find themselves sinking hours into online conversations without results related to their jobs.

> *In one scenario, the community might help your staff be more efficient and effective. In another scenario, staff could find themselves sinking hours into online conversations without results related to their jobs.*

In the beginning, the hard work of setting up social spaces, setting policies, experimenting, and learning will take a lot of time—and it will take a while before your staff members learn how to avoid the second sce-

Open Community Means Developing Into a Social Organization . 73

nario (time suck) in favor of the first (truly leveraging the community). But that time is an investment in a future where social media will be taken for granted. You're creating the infrastructure you need in your organization to be a part of your own online community. Is there another choice? We're going to assume you said "no" or "not really" and continue on.

The other important point is that the time factor will ebb and flow; once you get the community going and the infrastructure in place, maintaining it and managing the community can take less time overall. Then you might need another big push before an annual conference or during a fundraising or advocacy campaign of some kind.

GET TO THE POINT ALREADY.

- Building Open Community using social media has implications for how we work in terms of individual behaviors and skill sets, internal processes and communications channels, and organizational culture, where hierarchies are flattened and boundaries are blurred between official and unofficial spokespersons.

- Social organizations have traits that make them better at building and managing community online—they are more open, decentralized, fearless, and collaborative. Setting up an internal framework for managing community—a social media team and task forces to work on specific projects in a collaborative environment—will help you build the capacity to become a more social organization.

- Go for clarity over control. Ensure everything starts with the association's mission, that everyone knows what they are trying to achieve and what their roles are in making that reality. Establish clear policies. Define internal responsibilities. Manage internal communications about social media work so that silos and hierarchies become less important.

- Rethink your role as a publisher. Everyone's a publisher. You need to do it better. Go for speed over perfection. Rethink the value of your content. Do the Google test, and figure out how to repackage content to fuel your community's interest in your unique content that really is worth paying for.

- Develop your staff's skills so that they can have more meaningful interactions with your community. Your staff will represent you, even as the lines between personal and professional interactions will become harder to draw. It all comes down to trust. A full-time community manager can be a great asset, but ultimately everyone in the organization needs to figure out how their work interacts with the community.

CHAPTER 3

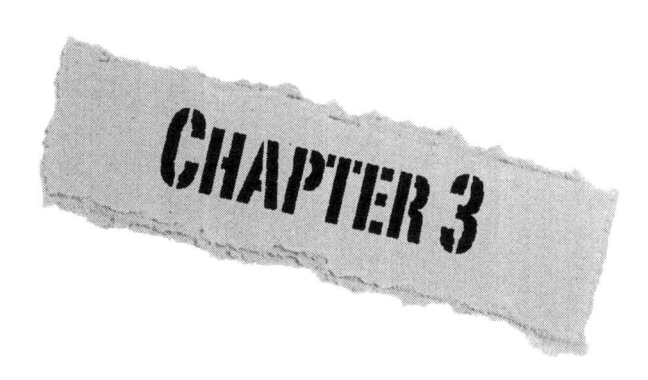

Open Community Means Embracing the Ecosystem

I had that dream again where I found a web app that would solve all of humanity's problems, and then forgot to bookmark it.

There's something to be said for the mess.

Wouldn't it be great if you could set up a single website where all the members of your community would come and spend all of their time together under the auspices of your organization? We've heard some technology vendors make this promise in the past. Build your own social network with the right technology infrastucture, and you'll no longer be at the mercy of the chaotic social web. You'll be in the driver's seat. You'll own all the data. You'll have all of the content. You'll be a true online "destination." And you'll be able to measure everything.

Unfortunately, building community online doesn't work that way. Sorry, but it's not about you, your website, or your tech infrastructure—no matter how tempting it might be to try to make it easy on yourself. It's about your people. And since no two people are alike, and passionate people have an irrepressible tendency to self-organize, there is simply no way to serve your entire community without accepting a little bit of messiness.

Messiness is our way of describing the potentially complicated ecosystem of your community. You'll have a homebase where you concentrate most of your efforts alongside outposts where you'll make it easier for your people to find you where they are already hanging out online. You'll have official spaces that you set up because they are directly serving your business objectives alongside unofficial spaces where your people are coming together on their own. You'll have spaces that are more public, spaces that are more private, and spaces that you may not even know exist. There will be spaces where you'll need to be very hands on, and spaces where it's better to be hands off. There will be certain people who participate in many of these spaces, and others who participate in a single space only.

> **Organizations that figure out what clarity over control means in their community will have the discipline to look past the messiness and see the beauty of the ecosystem.**

This stuff gets complicated. It's enough to make your head hurt. Then again, organizations that figure out what clarity over control means in their community will have the discipline to look past the messiness and see the beauty of the ecosystem. More importantly, they'll know how to keep that ecosystem healthy and fruitful.

Understand your role in the ecosystem.

"The organization is a substantial part of an ecosystem but not solely responsible for the health and growth of the entire system, and at the same time very dependent on the activities and health of parts of the system that are outside its sphere of control."
—Jamie Notter, vice president, organizational effectiveness, Management Solutions Plus[4]

In biology, the community—all of the organisms sharing an environment—is a part of the bigger ecosystem that encompasses all of the interrelated biological, physical, and chemical processes that create a stable system. In the context of Open Community, the ecosystem is a useful metaphor for understanding that the community you build around your organization online is a part of a larger system of social interactions and environmental factors experienced by the people in your community. In other words, the larger ecosystem affects your community. You can see this concept manifest in a thousand ways. Here are just a few ways that we've seen:

- A related profession with a vibrant online community takes an interest in a hot topic that your community is discussing. They pick up your community's discussion through their blogs, disputing a key point that had been taken for granted by your members.

- A natural disaster affects the life of one of your key influencers, and the online community rises to provide relief by encouraging everyone to donate through Network for Good.

- A group of people planning to attend an annual meeting realize through their Facebook connections that they all have school-aged kids. They decide to make the meeting a family trip and stay an extra day to take a trip together to see the sights. (Then the kids stay connected to each other on Facebook afterwards, too.)

None of these scenarios is particularly groundbreaking. You can imagine them happening in some form without the Internet. But when the scenarios unfold online, they are visible to you, and you can choose whether or not to take a more formal role in helping to organize or facilitate these interactions. You can decide whether to take these conversations that are happening at the periphery and share them with the heart of your Open Community.

Home(base) is where the heart is.

Think of your homebase as the heart of your messy community ecosystem. It's the place where you invest the most time and energy in serving your community. It's the place where people know they can find you and others in your community. Your homebase is also the place where you can be utterly clear about your organization's mission and day-to-day work.

> **homebase** *(noun)*
> A website serving as a central hub for an organization's digital content that is meant for distributing across the social web. A homebase often has social features such as RSS feeds, commenting, and sharing to public social networks.

A good homebase has a few important qualities:

- **Frequent updates.** Frequency is important because your homebase will feed and nurture your community. Ideally, your homebase should be updated at least daily. Organizations with a lot of content will likely publish even more often.

- **Two-way interaction.** Comments and conversations are what make the homebase about the community rather than just about you.
- **Openness.** This is a place where your staff is sharing information. Openness is important, both in terms of being clear about which staff persons are leading the conversations, and in terms of the kind of information you share.
- **Searchability.** Your homebase needs to have public content. And it needs to be easy to find from any search engine.
- **Shareability.** Along with searchability goes shareability. Content on your homebase should be interesting enough to pass along, either by email or through other social spaces like Facebook, Twitter, or LinkedIn.

A homebase can take a lot of different forms. It could be a blog, a whitelabel social network, even your main website can serve as a homebase if you build in these qualities. Your homebase should be where you host all kinds of shareable content. It should be the source for all the RSS feeds that pipe pieces of that content out to your outposts "automagically" (carried out automatically in such a clever way that the result appears to be magic[5]). Your homebase should have lots of dynamic content, and your community should be able to do all kinds of commenting, sharing, and discussing of your content right there—at home, so to speak. The more your community can come to you to find content and connect with one another, the more you'll be recognized as the glue that holds the community together.

Outposts are healthy.

Outposts are social spaces where your stakeholders are already interacting with each other online. An association might find its members and stakeholders gathering on Facebook, LinkedIn, Twitter, YouTube, Flickr, industry blogs, or other niche social spaces. Activity in an outpost can be official, meaning that a presence was deliberately created, or it can be unofficial, where group members self-organized without you.

If you can get a feel for your members who are gathering in outposts, you can meet them where they are and get them to re-engage with the community. And that's what makes outposts just as important as your homebase. The web is atomizing. It's no longer enough to have all of your content in one place; people expect content to come to them. Your community will have conversations where they happen, and it's important to be aware and supportive of those interactions.

Having official outposts is a way to provide a rallying point for your community. It's also a way for you to establish and promote your official voice and brand—another clarity over control point. Unofficial outposts might spring up around your association brand, but if your official outpost is better, your community will naturally gravitate toward the "real thing," especially when your group has more members and more frequent updates, making it rise to the top of search results. Some common examples of official outposts are staff-run Facebook Pages, LinkedIn Groups, and Twitter accounts.

Unofficial outposts often spring up to support niche small groups or to fill a void you may not even know exists. A few examples might be: a member-created Facebook Page, the blog for a popular industry publication, or a vendor-created LinkedIn group for an event you run. Unofficial outposts will constantly test the social boundaries of your organization. How can you monitor them? What if an unofficial outpost uses your logo? What if the admin is a critic? How much should you engage with them or offer to help? Sometimes unofficial outposts outperform the official outposts—in those cases, how can you reach out and reconnect with your self-organizing community?

"Any organization with a healthy community will have a mix of both official and unofficial outpost activity."

Any organization with a healthy community will have a mix of both official and unofficial outpost activity. That's a part of the messiness. Official outposts help your community identify you and others in the community. Unofficial outposts help them bond in new and surprising ways.

Create accidentally-on-purpose spokespersons.

Of course, one of the game-changing things about social media is that now anyone (staff, member, nonmember) can lead a conversation about the organization at any given moment. We have a tendency to fear this—what if someone says something controversial that is not the association's official position? But evangelizing by people who are not "official spokespersons" can be a powerful force for advancing the mission of the association, if only you can harness and direct that word of mouth. Many associations are seeing members go off and not only talk about their organization freely but also use and modify logos, branding, and messages. The social web has made it incredibly easy to go and create something (a group, a fan page, a website, anything) in the name of the association.

> "Evangelizing by people who are not 'official spokespersons' can be a powerful force for advancing the mission of the association."

And why not? The big shift here is to realize that this is a gift. A good thing. What if the opposite were true? What if the association had absolutely nothing that people wanted to talk about? No content they wanted to share with their friends and colleagues? If you have nothing worth mentioning, then maybe you shouldn't exist at all. How's that for a hard truth?

The phenomenon of the accidental spokesperson is a part of the messiness of building community online. A social organization sees opportunity in the enthusiasm of its fans. All of the traits of a social organization—openness, decentralization, fearlessness, and collaboration—instill the natural instinct for staff and volunteer community members to reach out to fans and welcome them into the larger ecosystem of the community and the organization. And if your online community spaces—your homebase and your outposts—are easy to find and join, you can go from "accidental spokespersons" to "accidentally-on-purpose spokespersons."

All community happens in small groups.

"Now that group-forming has gone from hard to ridiculously easy, we are seeing an explosion of experiments with new groups and new kinds of groups." —Clay Shirky, author of *Here Comes Everybody*[6]

How many people do you feel connected to? We mean really connected to. Now think about the last party you attended. Did everyone participate in a single conversation, each waiting his or her turn to speak? Or did everyone break off into groups of twos and threes and have their own animated conversations?

The larger your community becomes, the more important small groups become. Why? Because small groups are where the feeling of interconnectedness takes hold. This makes sense to associations, since we see these dynamics play out offline in our chapters, networks, special interest groups, and volunteer groups. Of course, groups spring into existence online far more easily than offline. Where once we had to do studies and surveys and meetings and more surveys to decide what groups we should form for our members, and then we had to figure out how our staff would support and administer those groups, now those same members can organize themselves organically around pretty much anything, including a discussion topic, a cause, an event, a location, or even hobbies and personal interests.

Groups are "ridiculously easy" to form but not necessarily easy to keep going. Sometimes they die when the interest in the topic dies. Sometimes they die because the champions who started them move on to some new project. Sometimes something newer and more exciting takes their place. This is part of the messiness. Traditionally when an association forms a group offline, so much has gone into the process of choosing, building, and maintaining that group that letting a group die is costly and heartbreaking. But when forming groups is so easy, no group is too precious to let die. They can come and go and come again to help your community feel more interconnected.

> **When forming groups is so easy, no group is too precious to let die. They can come and go and come again to help your community feel more interconnected.**

Create safe spaces.

"*The Dude abides.*" —The Dude, in *The Big Lebowski*[7]

Embracing the messiness does not mean standing by while your community goes hog wild. If you have clear, simple community guidelines that are posted somewhere where everyone can see them, you'll go a long way toward building safe spaces. Community guidelines allow your people to know when someone is misbehaving. Communities like rules, actually, and tend to be happily self-policing. Public social sites like Facebook, Twitter, and LinkedIn have their own posted terms of use in cases of serious issues, but that doesn't mean you can't set your guidelines, too, as long as they are simple and easy to abide by. This is your party; it's ok to say "no jumping on the furniture."

> **As an organization, your willingness to share ownership of your social spaces—and your openness to input from the people in those spaces about how the space should be shaped—is critical to your success at building your community online.**

You may find that your community needs slightly different sets of guidelines for different social spaces, such as Facebook (more social) or LinkedIn (more professional), but as with everything, the simpler you can keep the guidelines, the easier it will be for everyone to follow.

But here's the rub: if your community members don't like your guidelines, they don't have to accept them. They can go off and form their own groups without you. Always remember how "ridiculously easy" that is. As an organization, your willingness to share ownership of your social spaces—and your openness to input from the people in those spaces about how the space should be shaped—is critical to your success at building your community online.

Public and private spaces can coexist after all.

A debate that often crops up is about how public or private your community spaces should be. Even in corporate-owned outposts like LinkedIn and Facebook, you can make privacy decisions about who can join a group, what information will be only for group members, and what information will be visible to the public. And on your own website, you have even more privacy options. You can keep your entire community space behind a login, though we would very rarely recommend that as your best option.

Communities need a mix of public and private spaces to support the messiness. Think of a large conference as an analogy.

- Public spaces where a thought leader is featured = general session.

- Public spaces where everyone can interact = welcome party.

- Private spaces where anyone can join = breakout sessions.

- Private spaces that are invitation only = board meetings.

You might have certain groups of people who only feel comfortable in private spaces; CEOs, for example, often gravitate toward private spaces where they can interact with other CEOs. Others might need the public space; content creators, for example, often feel strongly that their work should reach the widest audience possible. The simplest thing to do is to ask different groups in your community what they need in terms of privacy, decide how their needs intersect with your business objectives, then set up your spaces accordingly.

Chapters and components are messy, too.

Many associations have a national or international hub and a number of chapter or component groups that are related to the hub. National and international organizations should consider active chapter community sites as important outposts. Of course, each local chapter's website or white-label social network will be their own homebase, linking together all their own outposts, including the national organization's spaces.

There has always been push and pull between national associations and their component groups. We've seen cases where the national association has led the efforts, bringing tools and mentorship to their components. We've also seen cases where one of the component groups jumped ahead with experiments of its own and brought the national organization along from its success. Both scenarios move the needle toward the goal of building community online, provided you recognize the overlap and find ways to collaborate.

Consider the scenario on the following pages for two related organizations.

Figure 1: National Homebase

This visualization shows the many social spaces where the people in one association's Open Community interact online. The social spaces emphasized in black are the homebase and official outposts that the association manages.

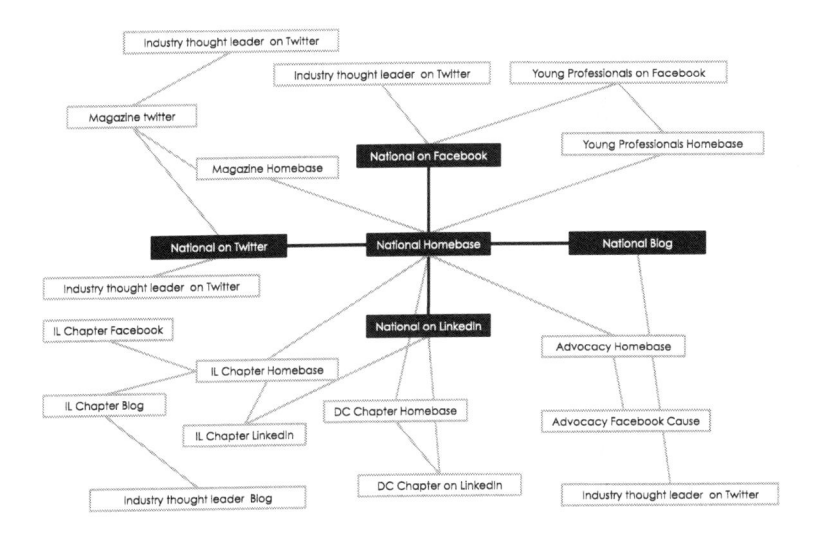

Open Community Means Embracing the Ecosystem

Figure 2: Illinois Chapter Homebase

In this visualization, the social spaces emphasized in black are the homebase and official outposts of the Illinois Chapter. Notice that the National Homebase is considered an important outpost by the chapter. Notice also that the larger ecosystem is the same for the national as it is for the chapter.

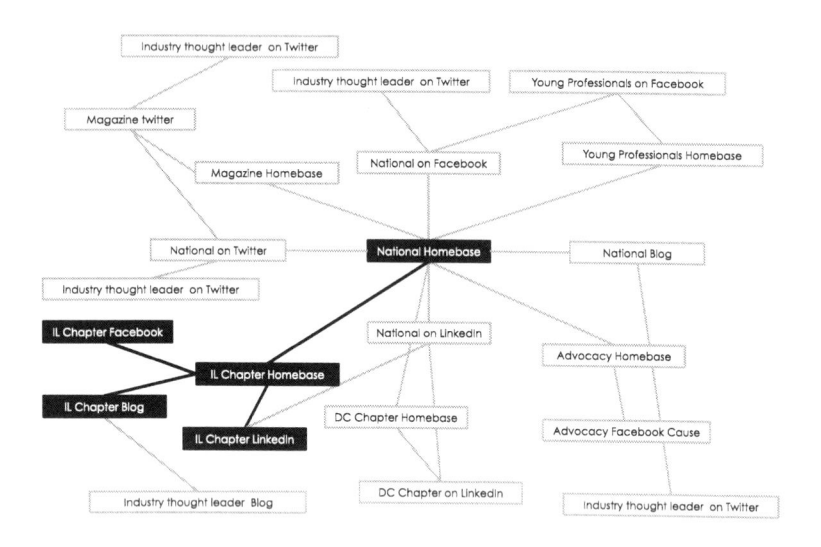

GET TO THE POINT ALREADY.

- Your community is going to be messy, so get used to it. To support the needs of your community online, you'll need the right mix of official and unofficial, public and private, homebase and outposts, hand on and hands off. The social organization is better poised to operate within this messy ecosystem.

- Your homebase is the central hub that enables your organization to interact with the community, no matter how messy it gets. This is the place where you can be completely clear as an organization about who you are, what you believe, and what you're doing to show for it.

- Outposts encompass all of the official and unofficial community activity that takes place away from your homebase. A healthy community will have a mix of official outposts, which give your community members a gathering place where they are already hanging out online, and unofficial outposts, where community members connect in ways that we might not have imagined.

- Accidental spokespersons are another part of the messiness of community online. While it's scary to imagine scenarios where accidental spokespersons misrepresent the organization, the more common scenario involves fans evangelizing your work to their peers. Look for ways to support your fans and create "accidentally-on-purpose spokespersons."

- All community happens in small groups, and every small group has unique needs. A big part of the messiness is creating safe spaces for different small groups. The right community guidelines for each social space are a start. You'll also want to consider how public or private different spaces should be.

- Associations with chapters and components need to figure out how to collaborate between national and local or special interest groups. Whether the national organization is the leader or a component group jumps ahead, learn from one another and recognize that you're serving overlapping communities online.

CHAPTER 4

Open Community Means Empowering the Periphery

I don't like this any more than you do. But the research clearly shows our members want to engage with us as the crew of a Klingon battle cruiser.

Is there an echo in here?

How often do you find yourself talking to the same core group of active members? You know them so well that you can predict how they might react to everything you're doing. You might even start to hear the same feedback over and over from the same people. But are your most vocal members truly representative of the rest of your community?

Open Community empowers the periphery, those silent members, new members, future members, industry leaders not yet in your membership, and plenty of other vaguely interested stakeholders at the edges of your community. Anyone who cares enough can now give you feedback and insight into his or her life. The social web promises to give us the ability to engage more people in more ways, but in order to fulfill that promise, we have to get to know our members and stakeholders—not just the folks we already know but also the folks we hope to know.

You might be thinking to yourself, "Wait a minute. Isn't there just as much of an echo chamber online, where the same people dominate the conversation?" Yes. Funny how offline life and online life are so similar, right? Open Community requires taking stock of a new diversity of voices, because it empowers anyone to be heard. It challenges you to acknowledge and incorporate feedback from the periphery. And it challenges you to rethink how value flows between all stakeholders and the organization.

Your community is not your database.

It's tempting to think that you can take your database, plug it into one of those cool social networking programs, and—voila!—online community. Nope. Doesn't work that way. Open community is in the connections, the interactions, the love that the people in your ecosystem share. You have people in your database who will never be a true part of your community online. And there are people who are not in your database (yet) who may end up being central to your community online.

That's not to say you can't use your database to help you understand the community you're trying to serve online. Associations know lots of useful things about members, such as their occupation, their age and gender, and their level of engagement with the association. You probably know a bit about their online habits, too. And you know what's most important to them, such as what kinds of information or opportunities get your members to click through on an email or what the most popular sections of your website are.

All that said, sometimes the best thing you can do is to forget what you know. For many associations, building community online opens up a lot of possibilities that members never imagined. Some of the assumptions staff have long held are breaking down—your members might just surprise you.

Get ready for the Social CRM.

Sometimes, members are willing to share information in a social networking setting that they wouldn't necessarily provide on a membership application. The information can help you understand members in new ways and develop your products and services (as well as your community online) to better serve them.

That's where the Social Customer Relationship Management (CRM) concept becomes compelling. Social CRM augments traditional customer relationship management processes with social networking data that is available from public sites and the organization's own private communities. Right now, for-profit companies are scrambling to figure out how to integrate Social CRM into their business processes. Associations will be fast followers, though we might rename the concept the "Social AMS," because the association management software systems will sit at the center of this movement. You can also see how this concept applies to donor management software systems.

"Imagine being able to pull up information that your members are sharing publically in real time."

Imagine being able to pull up information that your members are sharing publically in real time. For example, you see that a long-time member has not renewed her membership. You go to her profile and you see that she added a new job to her LinkedIn profile. The email you have is for her former company, but you can now pull the correct data over from her LinkedIn profile.

The Social CRM is not far off. Even now, you can go to companies like Rapleaf or Flowtown and get public data your members are sharing online. Start now to think about what kinds of data will be useful for you to know and how you can start collecting it. Here are a few ideas with possible scenarios.

- **Hobbies.** You've been running a golf tournament at your annual meeting, but now you see that you have just as many tennis players. You start a tennis group so they can self-organize at the event.

- **Education history.** You have a surprising number of graduates from the University of Michigan. You organize a Go Blue group online and set up a mentorship program with recent Michigan grads.

- **Job history.** You have a number of members who lost their jobs when a large company in your industry went bankrupt. You reach out to them and offer career assistance and free membership for the year.

- **URLs of public social sites** (personal blog, Twitter, Facebook, LinkedIn, for example). You find a lot more members have personal blogs than you knew. You create a blogger group and show them how to add their feeds to your website.

- **Mobile phone.** You learn that 20 percent of your members are now using iPhones. You decide to create an iPhone app with custom alerts related to advocacy.

- **Alternate email.** Your most active members are happy to give you their personal email addresses. Turns out that they've been on Facebook all along, and now you are able to invite them to your page.

Community unlocks useful data.

As you build your community online, you're going to learn a lot more about your members and potential members. The data you unlock can change the way you design and market your organization. Start now to look for ways to track these things:

- **Influence.** Identify and track the thought leaders and trendsetters who can raise awareness about your organization's programs and brand.

- **Engagement.** Track the online engagement of your members as an indicator of likelihood to renew or participate in events, for example.

- **Word of mouth.** Track your marketing efforts to see what promotions your community finds worth mentioning and which community members are driving conversions.

The first step is to decide what makes someone influential? What does meaningful engagement look like? What specific word-of-mouth topics are worth tracking? Once you know what you're looking for and what questions you're trying to answer, you'll find ways to track and measure.

Behavioral demographics: useful data you already have.

Behavioral demographics are a crucial and practical lens for viewing your community. You already know a lot about your members' daily life, right? When you're looking at ways to engage your community online, start with data you already have:

- Professional role within the industry.
- Demographics.
- Volunteer activities.
- Event participation.
- Professional interest areas.
- Engagement level.

In addition, find out what your data tells you about:

- Life stage.
- Digital orientation.
- Level of education.

These are very manageable datapoints for associations, especially groups that form around a profession. Are they just starting to get into the workforce? Are they getting married and having children? Are they focusing on mid-career professional development? Are they retiring soon? In all cases, there are great reasons for people to spend a lot of time online, but the way in which they do so will shift and change over time.

From creators to spectators and everyone in between.

> "When failure is cheap, sometimes a series of small experiments will give you the insight you need to move forward with confidence."

Just like daily life matters, so does digital life. Do you know how your members actually use the Internet? What kinds of online social actions do they naturally gravitate toward? Forrester Research has a useful way to categorize how people participate online using something it calls "social technographics."[8] Forrester defines social technographics as seven levels of participation in online activities: creators, conversationalists, critics, collectors, joiners, spectators, and inactives. Think about how your members fall into these levels, and what their preferences mean for the types of social spaces you can create.

The way we see it, there are three really good ways to find out how your members use the web:

1. **Listen and experiment.** When failure is cheap, sometimes a series of small experiments will give you the insight you need to move forward with confidence.

2. **Gather new data.** When members renew or register for events, ask them for the URLs of their social media profiles and blogs. Simple and effective.
3. **Survey.** You can add questions about online behavior to survey tools you already use. Or you can license the social technographics survey tools from Forrester and compare your membership to the U.S. population.

Are they spending time in front of a computer?

The particular field your organization represents is important. Are they doctors, seeing patients most of their work day? Are they administrators of some kind, more likely to be sitting in front of a computer all day? Are they contractors out on the road with just a smartphone to access email and the web? Are they educators in rural areas or isolated from their peers?

These are all real-life scenarios that different associations face. And none of these scenarios are deal breakers when it comes to online community. Understanding your members' real-life habits will help you understand why different community-building experiments fail or succeed. You might learn that you need to change the time of day you host a live chat. Or maybe you need a tool that's more mobile friendly. Or you might need specific features to help peers connect across long distances. The more you know about your members' daily life, the better you can design spaces, contexts, tools, and interactions. These nuances will make a big difference to how you will build your online spaces.

Generation matters, but not the way you'd think.

There's a lot of talk about generations these days. Generational differences do not provide clear answers or enough granularity to be able to use them to predict what people will do in your online space. Remember that the defined generations draw boundaries around something that actually exists on a continuum. And while we may be able to find truths there, it's like looking at the surface of the earth while standing on the moon.

Don't make the mistake of thinking that just because your members are mostly over 50 that they won't be interested in collaborating online. Based on data from public sites like Facebook and LinkedIn, social media adoption and use is rising rapidly for *all* generations. On Facebook, the fastest growing segment is the Boomer generation.[9]

> Where generation matters most is in the way you invite people into the community and how you nurture their involvement over time.

Where generation matters most is in the way you invite people into the community and how you nurture their involvement over time. Boomers may need clear objectives, regular walk-throughs, and storytelling about the power of the web to connect to a cause or mission or a group's particular goals.

Xers may need more autonomy, more creative input, and clear and open access to data and content. They'll need to really get a sense of what's in it for them and how they can use it their way. Millennials may need clear reasons to engage with your community when there are so many other ways for them to get information and collaborate with their peers online. They may also demand a richer operating environment. As an analogy, if they're used to World of Warcraft and you give them Pong, you've missed the mark.

It's not about technological savvy. It's about subtle differences in what each generation values, which ties back to historical trends when each generation was growing up. Generational trends won't give you the answer or tell you what to do, but if you learn more about the differences you will be able to more quickly understand trends in the behavior of your members and their particular demographic mix.[10]

It's not about age. It's about curiosity.

We've seen a lot of associations start Facebook Pages to reach their young professionals, only to find that the pages attract a mix of folks they never would have thought to connect with there. What do the people who connect with you online have in common? Curiosity.

You're looking for people who are always willing to try something new, to do things differently, to jump in with both feet. You're looking for people who get excited by possibilities and people who love to build things. Curiosity is not the exclusive domain of any one generation. In fact, the mixing of generations might just be the source of interest for some of those who are participating.

Part of building community online, then, is catering to the curious. They want the latest news without the slick PR spin. They want to try new tools occasionally. They want sneak peeks into whatever else your organization is working on. The more you can feed their curiosity, the more likely they are to stay engaged in the community.

Share the love with your digital extroverts.

Some people are just more willing to put themselves out there. That's true in real life, and it's true in online life. Digital extroverts are the vocal minority online who are hosting and participating in groups and conversations that have the potential to shape your industry (and your organization).

Digital extroverts (a term we love, coined by Brian Solis)[11] may have large personal networks (hundreds of friends on Facebook, 500 or more colleagues on LinkedIn, thousands of Twitter followers) but not always. Just as often they are thoughtful, well-respected professionals who are tightly bonded to fewer people. The more telling measurements of digital extroverts are how often they participate in conversations, comment in social spaces, and post updates to their social networks. They may or may not have their own blogs, but they're definitely out there engaging with others who do.

Get to know your digital extroverts, your "talkers," as Andy Sernovitz describes them in the book *Word of Mouth Marketing*.[12] Hopefully, they're members and fans of your organization. If not, find out why. If they are fans, invite them to help you shape your social media work to be meaningful for them. And give them something remarkable to talk about.

Find your champions.

"They are not bought, they extol your virtues freely. As your evangelist, they feel connected to something bigger than themselves." —Jackie Huba, coauthor of *Creating Customer Evangelists*[13]

To successfully build community online, you must first identify your champions. These are people who already—without being asked—sing your praises, talk to their colleagues and friends about your programs or services, or go above and beyond with their desire to volunteer their time and energy for you. Associations have lots of champions, or "customer evangelists," as Jackie Huba refers to them. For your online community, you need to find champions who are also digital extroverts—or champions who are curious enough to become digital extroverts.

" **For your online community, you need to find champions who are also digital extroverts— or champions who are curious enough to become digital extroverts.** "

Luckily, finding your online champions is easy. They're "liking" your Facebook Page, joining your LinkedIn group, following your Twitter account, and talking about your industry and organization in other social spaces online. They might even have their own groups on public social networks or their own blogs. They have online influence: a good number of friends, colleagues, and followers, and a willingness to share information that they feel is important.

It's really less about you finding champions as it is about champions finding you. If you're listening—both through keyword searches and through your network of industry thought leaders—you'll see champions emerge. And if you've set up a great homebase and a rich network of outposts intended to reach people where they're already hanging out, your champions will connect to you in any number of ways.

Who belongs?
It's your Open Community's call.

Your community has citizens, not to be confused with your association's members. Being a citizen of your association's Open Community means caring enough to take part and build meaning alongside fellow citizens. You likely have a lot of members who will never be citizens of your community. You might call them checkbook members, those who pay their dues but never actually participate. Equally, you potentially have a lot of citizens in your community who are not yet members.

The Open Community itself decides who is a citizen, not your membership records. It decides based on who actively contributes value to the community as a whole. This is especially true in public outposts like Twitter, Facebook, and LinkedIn. As your community develops, you'll uncover a pretty big, complex matrix of overlapping and adjacent relationships. It's that interconnectedness and the personal identity that it creates that lead someone to feel like a citizen of your community.

Citizens versus members.

"Community is built not by specialized expertise, or great leadership, or improved services; it is built by great citizens." —Peter Block, author of *Community: The Structure of Belonging*[14]

Here's the rub. Citizens who are not (yet) members can bring just as much (and sometimes more) value to the online community and the association as a whole compared to long-time members who are not present online. We believe this paradox will lessen over time as social tools become mundane and the percentage of members who are not interacting online becomes negligible. But we're not there yet.

How do citizens bring value? Maybe they are creating content. Maybe they're leading discussions. Maybe they're using their influence to bring in more people who care about your industry. How valuable is that engagement? If your goal is to build community online, and you believe Peter Block's idea that community is built by great citizens, than you really cannot undervalue the gifts of all of your community's citizens, regardless of their membership status.

The nature of Open Community begs you to ask some tough questions about who your association serves, what value the community drives, and what the association can bring to the table that the community can't drive on its own.

You may need to look at your membership model through a new lens. What would happen if membership were driven by a citizen's contributions rather than dues? At this stage, these conversations may be more philosophical than practical, but they are still worth having.

GET TO THE POINT ALREADY.

- Getting to know your members online is about more than data. Your community is not your database, and there is no shortcut to building community using your data. That said, data can help you make better decisions about how best to build your community to serve your members.

- Prepare your organization for the day when your AMS can include social data from public sites. The Social AMS will give you insight into your members that you can use to build community, and as you build your community you'll unlock useful data that members might not have thought to share with you otherwise.

- Behavioral demographics and social technographics are useful in understanding the daily life and online habits of your members. Things that seem obvious—how much time they spend in front of a computer and what generation they belong to—can be trumped by your members' curiosity and willingness to experiment.

- Champions and digital extroverts will be at the core of your community. Finding them and engaging with them is simply a matter of listening and being present.

- Citizenship means caring enough about your community to take part and build meaning alongside fellow citizens. Citizens are defined by their interconnectedness and contributions to the community, not by their membership status. The concept of citizenship separate from membership brings up a lot of questions about value and dues that are worth discussing, if only in theory for the time being.

CHAPTER 5

Open Community Means Participant-Defined Engagement

We accidentally sent a message to our evangelists instead of our influencers, and now our advocates and change agents are at each others' throats!

Hurdles along the path to engagement.

As association executives, we understand the process of developing our membership. We work to cultivate our relationships with members, and we look for ways to move members along a path of engagement, from prospective member, to brand new member, to active member, to volunteer leader, to board member.

Your community online, just like your community offline, has its own path of engagement. Our job is to remove the hurdles that keep people from becoming more engaged. So what are the hurdles along the way?

- **Finding you online.** How easy is it to find your community online? Put yourself in the place of someone who doesn't know you online—or better yet, someone who doesn't know you at all. This is where having a messy community and a big ecosystem can be an advantage.

- **Knowing how to participate.** How easy is it to participate? Are there onerous sign-up processes? Are the tools tricky? Is your community "cliquey"? Does one have to be a member first?

- **Feeling connected.** How easy is it to personally connect with members of the community? Are there ways for people to form close bonds with one another and feel closer to the community as a whole because of those bonds? Are you enabling those small groups to form and thrive?

- **Feeling invested.** The last hurdle, and perhaps the hardest to get over, feeling invested is the difference between being a citizen of the community and being a true champion of the community.

Your community will naturally be made up of people who are new to the community, people who have been around a while, people who are very actively engaged, and people who are champions. There will also be people who are essentially dormant within it, or folks who reached a hurdle and gave up. Think about how you can move people along the path of engagement and maybe lower a few hurdles for those folks who decided it was all too much.

Member to member trumps staff to member.

Having people in your community who feel connected and invested—having champions—is critical. And when you're just starting out, your champions are the first people you should connect with. Why? For one thing, they're the most likely to respond and the most likely to be patient as you build your community online. But the biggest reason is this: members are far more likely to respond to a request from a fellow member than from association staff. Members listen to each other. They trust each other. The organization needs to create social spaces where that trust can be shared freely inside its community, member to member, citizen to citizen.

> "The organization needs to create social spaces where trust can be shared freely inside its community, member to member, citizen to citizen."

So here are the questions that will drive you: How can you create more champions? How can you focus their energy and power? How can you be more open with them? How can you recognize their contributions? How can you create more champions? (Yes, we repeated that one on purpose.)

Champions are the key to scaling your community online. As staff, you simply cannot be everywhere all the time, nor should you be. You need the support of champions all over the web—in all the small groups and messy ecosystems—and you need the number of champions to grow in proportion to the size of your community.

Schmoozing your champions.

If you don't know your champions personally, get to know them by interacting with them wherever they are. Go ahead, do a little schmoozing. Tell them how much you appreciate the time and effort they are putting in. Comment on their posts. Retweet their links. Engage them in conversation. Then invite them to help you beta test, then soft launch, then fully launch, your community building efforts. Approach them like you would any volunteer—with an individual invitation and a clear outline of how you'd like them to help.

One way we like to do this is to create a special, private group just for champions. You do this offline when you create boards and committees. But your champions group is different. You're recognizing they are the linchpins of your community online, and you're creating a space where you can interact with them more openly than you might in other spaces:

- Ask for their frank feedback in a space where they might feel more free to be honest.

- Give them a sneak peek of projects you're working on while there is still time to change direction if they recommend it.

- Loop them in on upcoming campaigns first, and ask them to help you spread the word organically through word-of-mouth channels.

And for their part, the champions can talk amongst themselves about their passion for the community and how they'd like to contribute moving forward.

The role of the champion.

The beauty of the social web is that it enables more and more people to be champions for you in lots of different ways as the community flourishes. Your champions might:

- Act as a welcoming committee, helping newbies feel comfortable in what could otherwise be an intimidating, new experience.

- Seed the community by building user-generated-content, leading discussions, or posting photos.

- Nurture the community by replying to other members' posts.

- Spread the word about your community in both online and real-life interactions.

- Beta test new tools you introduce to your community and give valuable feedback.

- Defend the values and brand of your organization, should it ever come into question.

Getting citizens invested in your organization.

Before they became champions, they were citizens. Being a citizen has all the implications of wanting to participate: to give money and time or to be a content creator, "sharer," or commenter. It also has all the implied interactions inherent in being part of a group: the networking, the social, the face-to-face events, the learning, the professional development, the leadership, the belonging, the responsibility.

So how do you bring your citizens over the hurdle of feeling invested? How do you make them champions? You connect with their passion.

This is where the work you do as an organization—your mission and all of the fantastic programs, services, and products you provide to fulfill that mission—come in to play. As a social organization, how do you make the work you do connect with the passion of your citizens? Offline, you create volunteer opportunities such as special interest groups, local networks, PACs, certification bodies, and more. These used to work well, but you might be seeing participation shrink, or you might be stuck with some groups that people are no longer passionate about. While recreating all of this legacy structure online may make sense for helping your team with the work of administering all of these volunteer groups, it is not the right approach for igniting the passion of your online citizens and transforming them into champions. (Otherwise they'd already be champions, right?)

Rethink what it means to engage with your organization. How can you use social technologies to involve the citizens of your online community in new and exciting ways? How can you involve your citizens who are writers and teachers but aren't necessarily interested in committee work? What are the pieces of your work that will inspire passion from your community?

This is hard, and it takes creativity, openness to change, and a certain selflessness. A lot of times the work that would most inspire your citizens is the same work that inspires your staff: choosing a theme for the annual conference, picking artwork for the cover of your magazine, picking the best articles to be published in your magazine, covering an industry event for the community, speaking to a senior political leader. Your staff has to be willing to share some control over their work with the citizens of the community who are most passionate about various aspects of the organization.

Adhocracy and Volunteerism 2.0.

"The majority of members who say they volunteer for their association do so in adhoc jobs or on an as-needed basis. An 'adhocracy' volunteer model facilitates and rewards these volunteers, who remain greatly unrecognized in more traditional models. —Peggy Hoffman, president, Mariner Management & Marketing[15]

When you start to create new ways for your citizens to engage with the work of the organization, you can start to think about how building community online might change volunteerism within your organization.

adhocracy *(noun)*
A volunteer model that emphasizes flexible volunteering in non-permanent, one-at-a-time stints.[16] (Note: The term is an adaptation of the concept presented in *Adhocracy*, by Robert H. Waterman, Jr.,[17] and its use to describe volunteer models was popularized in the late 1980s by Nancy Macduff of *Volunteer Today*.)[18]

In the age of the social web, people want to be able to define how they volunteer, including when, for how long, and to what extent. Citizens can become champions when they join formal volunteer groups, but they can also become champions when they begin to regularly take on smaller, drop-in volunteer opportunities centered around their true passions. Your online spaces can be where you enable "raise your hand" volunteerism, where you have a place for people to find drop-in volunteer opportunities or even generate them on your behalf, and where people can form groups around specific tasks or causes and then let them fade when the purpose is fulfilled. For the first time, associations can use social tools to get out of the way and enable adhocracy within their communities. If someone wants to be engaged and you have a space for that to happen, you're creating champions by getting citizens more invested in your organization.

By the way, helping to build the community is itself a volunteer opportunity. When you ask citizens to help shape the community online, focusing on what's truly important to them, you are knocking down the hurdle of investment.

Connect online interactions to face-to-face interactions.

Face-to-face events are another way to knock down the hurdles of connectedness and investment. Online and face-to-face go together like peanut butter and chocolate. When people meet online, they look for a time and place to meet in person. There's just something about shaking hands and looking each other in the eye that cannot be replicated digitally. Connectedness can start online, but it's sealed in person.

On the other hand, how many times have you attended an event, only to return home and never again speak to the people you met for the first time? And what about your first-time attendees who know hardly anyone? In these cases, face-to-face alone is not enough to create connectedness. When those same people return home and connect online with people they first met face to face, there's a much better chance that they'll stay in touch with each other and your Open Community.

"When those same people return home and connect online with people they first met face to face, there's a much better chance that they'll stay in touch with each other and your Open Community."

Open Community Means Participant-Defined Engagement . 135

When you're working year-round to build and nurture your Open Community, you can connect people face to face in lots of different ways. Pretty much anytime two or more people who are connected to you come together, you can help keep them connected through your Open Community. Small, regularly scheduled happy hours and networking groups are great for building community on the local level. Community happens in small groups, after all. Large annual meetings are great for building community across geographical boundaries. Your Open Community can even meet up at events that are hosted by your sister (or competing) organizations.

The simplest thing that could possibly work.

"A complex system that works is invariably found to have evolved from a simple system that worked. The inverse proposition also appears to be true: A complex system designed from scratch never works and cannot be made to work. You have to start over, beginning with a working simple system." —John Gall, author of *Systematics: How Systems Really Work and How They Fail*[19] (The rule of thumb is often called "Gall's Law")[20]

Knowing how to participate is important. If the tools are too tricky, the processes too onerous, or the community too opaque, you've put up a hurdle that is too high for your potential citizens to jump. The answer is simplicity. Simplicity is hard to achieve, but it's crucial to building community online.

Take the lesson from Twitter: here's a very simple social space with an even simpler way to participate: simply answer the question "What's happening?" (This prompt changed from "What are you doing?" in November 2009.)[21] But Twitter doesn't represent a tiny basic community. It's huge. People have built their own meaning around this simple platform, and thousands of add-on applications have sprung up to add functionality. People have found hundreds of different ways to use it, personally and professionally, but its core simplicity is still there.

Simplicity is especially hard for associations, because we want to be everything to everyone. We tend to add features and programs and services in order to accommodate requests, without removing those that may not be relevant anymore. Associations started out simple, of course. Each started as a core group of people with like interests and a mission. But as they grew, those interests spread themselves out to accommodate larger groups of people. Go back to the mission. The mission is key. What is the simplest thing you can do to support that mission in your community online? Focus on that as your platform, and let everything else spring organically from there.

What's your association's social object?

"The fallacy is to think that social networks are just made up of people. They're not; social networks consist of people who are connected by a shared object." —Jyri Engeström, entrepreneur, angel investor at Social Objects[22]

Social objects are what your community revolves around, the content that will inspire your community members to have a social interaction with each other and not someone else. To figure out your social objects, answer the "now what?" question: "OK, so someone has logged in to the site, *now what*? What are they there for?"

> *"What can your members get from your social spaces that they can't get anywhere else? If you can't answer that question, start over."*

---

social object *(noun)*
A piece of content that draws people into social interactions. (Based on Jyri Engeström's object-centered sociality theory.)[23]

Open Community Means Participant-Defined Engagement . 139

For example, match these social objects to the sites that they fit best:

1. Jobs	A. Amazon
2. Friends	B. LinkedIn
3. Photos	C. Yelp
4. Videos	D. Facebook
5. Books	E. YouTube
6. Restaurants	F. Flickr

(1A, 2D, 3F, 4E, 5A, 6C—and if you see some overlap, you're not wrong!)

You may be thinking, "How can our site(s) be boiled down to just one social object, when we have different people doing different things?" It's not easy, but it's worth thinking about. It doesn't have to be just one, and you may have different social objects in different social spaces where your community gathers. Perhaps it's referrals. Perhaps it's learning groups for your credentialing program (or certification, standards, or accreditation). Perhaps it's articles from industry publications. Perhaps it's committee work. Perhaps it's pictures and videos from an annual conference. Perhaps it's member-generated articles or blog posts. Narrow it down to your core reason(s) for existing.

The most important question is this: What can your members get from your social spaces that they can't get anywhere else? If you can't answer that question, start over.

Social objects need social actions.

" *I believe that thinking about design from an activity-centric viewpoint is the most efficient way to get where you need to go… which is to create* ~~a piece of software~~ <u>an Open Community</u> *that is valuable to people.*" —Joshua Porter, author of *Designing for the Social Web*. (Edit is ours.)[24]

Social objects should always be accompanied by the option to take social action; otherwise, they're just objects and not so social. Having clear social actions is also a way to lower the barrier of participation. Knowing your social objects and the actions you want people to take with them can also help you choose the best public or private social spaces for your association. Think about the actions that are the most important for your social objects.

- If you're trying to connect people, than maybe joining, sharing, and "friending" are most important.

- If you're trying to curate content for your industry, maybe rating, reviewing, and commenting are most important.

- If you're trying to increase your association's visibility, maybe reposting on outposts or social bookmarking is most important.

This is where all the time you spent getting to know your community and their online behavior can really be valuable. For example, if your members are analytical and like to rate and review content, you might focus on that aspect of engagement as opposed to asking them to generate the content through blogging or uploading articles. Enable your potential citizens to do in your social spaces what they're already happy to do elsewhere.

The "what" trumps the "where."

It's more important to enable the social objects and actions of your community than it is to come up with a single, centralized place for them to convene. Certain tools do certain things better than others, and citizens want the best tool for the job. Think about all of the things your online community could want to accomplish together. You might brainstorm a myriad of possibilities. Here are some examples we've drawn from our work:

- **Engaging volunteers.** With volunteer opportunities as the social object, a private community can enable volunteers to recruit one another.

- **Collaboration and advocacy.** With stories and case studies as the social object, a public wiki can enable citizens to contribute stories from their work.

- **Influence and marketing.** With breaking industry news as the social object, outposts like Twitter, Facebook, and LinkedIn (along with Digg, for good measure) enable citizens to spread the word on your behalf.

- **Advocacy.** With the association's position on upcoming legislation as a social object, an association blog enables citizens to discuss the finer details and share their own stories with legislators.

- **Professional development.** With study groups as the social object, an online discussion forum with a live chat or webinar tool can enable volunteers to study online or even plan in person meet-ups.

Gifts from the community deserve thank-you notes.

When people put themselves on the line to contribute something to the community—maybe one posts a photo, writes a blog post, reviews an article or even becomes a community champion—they are contributing gifts to their fellow community members. It's important that contributors feel like their gifst have reach and impact.

Gifts that citizens contribute to the community help to build their reputations. Citizens and champions who have built great reputations will get more recognition for their gifts; people know them, trust them, and look for their contributions. Newer folks who are just beginning to build their reputation will not be so lucky. Their gifts might go largely unnoticed. That's a problem.

People who are new to the community need a little extra encouragement and gratitude to make them feel that their gifts are meaningful. Silence is deadly to community. If someone takes the time to contribute content to the community, and it is met by silence, that person is less likely to take the time to contribute again. Sounds like a job for champions and staff, right? Short of writing thank you-notes, there are a lot of ways to help everyone in your community build their reputations.

Reputation matters.

Reputation is the currency of community. Every time a person contributes to the community, that person is staking his or her reputation on the value of that contribution. In the early stages of building community online, your champions are staking a lot. Every time they invite a colleague, post content, add a comment, or create a group, they are using their reputations to enhance your community and betting that your community will be valuable to their peer group.

"*Every time they invite a colleague, post content, add a comment, or create a group, your champions are using their reputations to enhance your community.*"

The goal, then, is to turn the tables. You want participating in your community to enhance the reputations of your citizens and champions, making it more attractive for others to ramp up their own participation.

There are certain components you might add to a social object or member profile that are directly tied to reputation. No matter what the piece of content is, these components make a huge difference:

- Name and photo of the contributor.
- Date contributed (most recent tends to be most important).
- Ratings and reviews.
- Number of views, comments, likes, or retweets.
- Number of friends or followers of the contributor.
- Engagement points and flair for the contributor.

Engagement points and reputation flair.

"I don't really like talking about my flair."
—Joanna, in *Office Space*[25]

Engagement points and flair are a construct of the gaming world that have become a popular tactic on online community sites. Just like in a game, you score points, win powers, gather badges, and "level-up," so can you earn engagement points and flair to reflect your reputation in the community. We've seen a lot of different types of reputation flair, from simple labels that mark someone as a "champion" or "superstar" to images of ribbons very similar to what you might find at a conference or tradeshow. Communities created around events frequently designate speakers, sponsors, and exhibitors; that's a kind of reputation flair, too.

What makes this concept especially interesting is that no matter what, everyone who contributes to the community is earning some type of credit each and every time he or she contributes. And if you're very clear about how points and flair are earned, you may find people actually working toward flair goals.

This brings up some very interesting questions for your association. How do you define engagement, and how might you weight contributions in terms of points? Should citizens earn more points for contributing a blog post than they do for joining your annual meeting group? How might offline engagement factor in? If your ultimate goal for showcasing reputation is helping folks along the path of engagement, be sure to make it easy to progress. Remember you're trying to remove hurdles, not add new ones.

GET TO THE POINT ALREADY.

- Engaging your community is about removing the hurdles that keep people from participating. The first hurdle is finding you online. The second hurdle is knowing how to participate. Next comes feeling connected and, finally, feeling invested.

- Members will always respond better to requests from other members. That's why it's so important to start by connecting to champions, first. Then ask the champions to help you get the next wave of citizens participating in the community.

- You can give your champions very specific roles and tasks. They can welcome newbies, add content, lead discussions, reply to posts, spread the word, and test new tools. It's important to communicate exactly what you'd like your champions to do, because they're happy to help when they have clear instructions.

- The last hurdle, getting citizens to feel invested in your community, can only be overcome by tapping into a citizen's passion. Associations have a lot of ways to do this. One of the most compelling ways is to redefine what it means to be a volunteer. Enabling face-to-face interaction is another way.

- Simplicity is the best way to help citizens overcome the hurdle of knowing how to participate. Your association will need clear, unique social objects, and obvious social actions around those objects. Rather than trying to make a single tool work for everything, choose tools that are appropriate for the work that your citizens are trying to accomplish.

- Getting feedback from the community helps citizens feel connected. Unfortunately, people who are already connected and have built their reputations in the community naturally get more feedback. It's important for association staff and champions to make sure that citizens who are newer or less connected also get feedback so they can feel that their contributions have value. There are lots of ways to do this. For example, many white-label online community sites adapt gaming concepts; members earn engagement points for specific actions, and "flair" or profile badges based on the points enhance their reputations in the community.

152 . Open Community

CONCLUSION

Your Community Awaits

This isn't really a conclusion. It actually might be a starting point for some of you. For many we see it simply as a continuation of your journey, and we know there is much to be done. We hope that you've picked up a mix of ideas, ranging from very practical to a bit pie-in-the-sky. Pie is good sometimes.

The one thing we haven't done yet is celebrate you. (We kinda wanted to see if you'd make it this far before giving you the pat on the back that you so clearly deserve.) We're going to assume that you're passionate about your association community and that you're passionate about the possibilities of social technologies. That's why you read this book. That's why you're going to take the concepts of Open Community and work to incorporate them back in your day-to-day work. We know what you're facing, and we know that it takes courage, patience, and limitless optimism when it's much easier to be negative.

A big part of our job is "therapy" for organizations. We help them face fear and resistance to change. We help them struggle through personnel issues and leadership challenges. We help them weigh the risks and put some safety nets in place. We've been through this community stuff, and it's tough. Know that we feel your pain. We support your vision.

We want you, your team, and every citizen in your community to succeed.

And so, we invite you to join the conversations happening around this book at *http://opencommunitybook.com*. We hope that you'll come, share your stories, and connect with other readers of this book who are facing similar challenges. We'll use this site to dig deeper into all of the "big ideas" in this book. You'll be able to:

- See how several prominent association executives answer the question, "How will Open Community change associations?"

- Browse the web bibliography, with links to the most relevant posts from a variety of experts whom we respect.

- Get tools for presenting the concepts from this book to your staff.

One last thing. Through everything, believe in yourself and your ability to build Open Community for your organization, one step at a time. ***Go forth and be social!***

APPENDIX

Here are just a few of the books we love that can help you dig deeper into the ideas presented in this book.

- *Groundswell: Winning in a World Transformed By Social Technologies,* by Josh Bernoff and Charlene Li
- *Here Comes Everybody: The Power of Organizing Without Organizations,* by Clay Shirky
- *Creating Customer Evangelists: How Loyal Customers Become a Volunteer Sales Force,* by Ben McConnell and Jackie Huba
- *Word of Mouth Marketing: How Smart Companies Get People Talking,* by Andy Sernovitz
- *Community: The Structure of Belonging,* by Peter Block
- *Open Leadership,* by Charlene Li

Ideas around Open Community are evolving too fast for print. The best way to continue learning about this topic is to join the many conversations happening online, starting with the association and social media blogosphere. Here are a few of the blogs we recommend.

- *SocialFishing (http://www.socialfish.org/blog)* - our own blog, where the ideas from this book have been percolating for years.

- *Acronym (http://blogs.asaecenter.org/Acronym/)* - the required first stop in the association blogosphere.

- *Beth's Blog: How Nonprofits Can Use Social Media (http://www.bethkanter.org/)* - Beth Kanter on "how networked nonprofits are using social media to power change."

- *Convince and Convert (http://www.convinceandconvert.com/)* - consultant Jay Baer digs into corporate use of social media; good lessons for associations.

- *Get Me Jamie Notter - (http://www.getmejamienotter.com/)* - Jamie Notter digs deep into what makes a social organization. Monthly guest blogger at SocialFish.

- *The Harte of Marketing (http://www.theharteofmarketing.com)* - Beth Harte on "marketing and communications for the customer-centric organization."

- *John Haydon (http://www.johnhaydon.com/)* - John Haydon discusses "social media marketing for nonprofits" and provides all you need to know regarding social media tactics and implementation. Monthly guest blogger at SocialFish.

- *Smartblog Insights (http://smartblogs.com/insights/)* - "news and best practices from association, marketing and nonprofit leaders."

ENDNOTES

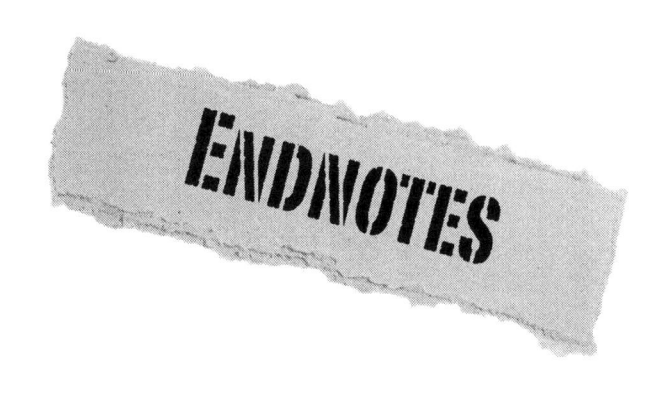

1. Wikipedia, Open community, *http://en.wikipedia.org/wiki/Open_community* (July 21, 2010).

2. Wikipedia, Gall's law, *http://en.wikipedia.org/wiki/Gall%27s_law* (July 21, 2010).

3. Voltaire, "La Bégueule," 1772, Wikiquote, *http://en.wikiquote.org/wiki/Voltaire* (July 22, 2010).

4. Jamie Notter, "Organizations in the Digital Age," SocialFish blog, March 24, 2010 *(http://www.socialfish.org/2010/03/organizations-in-the-digital-age.html)*.

5. Wiktionary, Automagic, *http://en.wiktionary.org/wiki/automagic* (July 21, 2010).

6. Clay Shirky, Here Comes Everybody: The Power of Organizing Without Organizations (Penguin, 2008), 54.

7. The Big Lebowski, dir. Joel Coen, writ. Joel Coen, Ethan Coen, perf. Jeff Bridges, Polygram, 1998.

8. Josh Bernoff, "Social Technographics: Conversationalists get onto the ladder" Groundswell blog, January 19, 2010 *(http://forrester.typepad.com/groundswell/2010/01/conversationalists-get-onto-the-ladder.html)*.

9. Michael Rogers, "Boomers and Technology: An Extended Conversation," AARP, October 28, 2009 *(http://www.aarp.org/technology/innovations/info-10-2009/boomers_and_technology.html)*.

    Peter Corbett, "Facebook Demographics and Statistics Report 2010," istrategylabs blog, January 4, 2010 *(http://www.istrategylabs.com/2010/01/facebook-demographics-and-statistics-report-2010-145-growth-in-1-year/)*.

10. Jamie Notter, Generational Diversity in the Workplace: Hype Won't Get You Results (Notter Consulting, 2007).

11. Brian Solis, "Breaking News: Twitter Debuts New Front Page," Brian Solis blog, July 28, 2009 *(http://www.briansolis.com/2009/07/breaking-news-twitter-debuts-new-front-page/)*.

12. Andy Sernovitz, Word of Mouth Marketing: How Smart Companies Get People Talking (Kaplan, 2009).

13. Ben McConnell, Jackie Huba, Creating Customer Evangelists: How Loyal Customers Become a Volunteer Sales Force (Kaplan, 2003), 2.

14. Peter Block, Community: The Structure of Belonging (ReadHowYouWant, 2009), 65.

15. Peggy M. Hoffman, CAE, "Adhocracy Defined: A Better Volunteer 'Mousetrap,'"Idea Center blog, May 13, 2010 *(http://www.marinermanagement.com/ideacenter/20100513/adhocracy-defined-a-better-volunteer-mousetrap)*.

16. Wikipedia, Adhocracy Movement, *http://en.wikipedia.org/wiki/Adhocracy_Movement* (July 21, 2010).

17. Robert H. Waterman, Jr., Adhocracy: The Power to Change (W. W. Norton & Co., 1993).

18. Volunteer Today, *http://www.volunteertoday.com* (July 22, 2010).

19. John Gall, Systemantics: How Systems Work and Especially How They Fail (Quadrangle, 1977).

20. http://en.wikipedia.org/wiki/Gall%27s_law

21. Biz Stone, "What's Happening," Twitter blog, November 19, 2009 *(http://blog.twitter.com/2009/11/whats-happening.html)*.

22. Jyri Engeström, "Why some social network services work and others don't — Or: the case for object-centered sociality," April 13, 2005 *(http://www.zengestrom.com/blog/2005/04/why-some-social-network-services-work-and-others-dont-or-the-case-for-object-centered-sociality.html)*.

23. *http://www.zengestrom.com/blog/2005/04/why-some-social-network-services-work-and-others-dont-or-the-case-for-object-centered-sociality.html*

24. Joshua Porter, "Activity-Centered Design," Bokardo blog, September 25, 2008 *(http://bokardo.com/archives/activity-centered-design/).*

25. Office Space, dir. Mike Judge, writ. Mike Judge, perf. Jennifer Aniston, Fox, 1999.

About the Authors

Maddie Grant, CAE, and Lindy Dreyer are association/nonprofit bloggers on social media strategy and marketing, community building, and innovation. Maddie worked as administrative director/COO for a professional membership association for several years, and Lindy was an agency marketer working for association clients until they launched their social media strategy consulting firm, SocialFish *(www.socialfish.org)*, which helps associations and nonprofits build Open Community on the social web.

Made in the USA
Lexington, KY
06 March 2011